Joel Dorman Steele

Manual of Science for Teachers

Containing Answers to the Practical Questions and Problems in the Author's

Scientific Text Books

Joel Dorman Steele

Manual of Science for Teachers
Containing Answers to the Practical Questions and Problems in the Author's Scientific Text Books

ISBN/EAN: 9783337279615

Printed in Europe, USA, Canada, Australia, Japan

Cover: Foto ©Paul-Georg Meister /pixelio.de

More available books at **www.hansebooks.com**

OF

SCIENCE FOR TEACHERS

CONTAINING

ANSWERS TO THE PRACTICAL QUESTIONS
AND PROBLEMS IN THE AUTHOR'S
SCIENTIFIC TEXT-BOOKS

BY

J. DORMAN STEELE, Ph.D., F. G. S.

AUTHOR OF THE FOURTEEN-WEEKS SERIES IN NATURAL SCIENCE

REVISED EDITION

TO ACCOMPANY THE POPULAR PHYSICS, POPULAR CHEMISTRY, HYGIENIC
PHYSIOLOGY, AND NEW DESCRIPTIVE ASTRONOMY

NEW YORK ·:· CINCINNATI ·:· CHICAGO
AMERICAN BOOK COMPANY

PREFACE.

SINCE the publication of the former edition of this Manual, Steele's Physics and Chemistry have been thoroughly revised, and the Hygienic Physiology has been published. The present issue has been prepared to accompany these later editions, and includes complete reference to all the problems and practical questions contained in Steele's Popular Physics, Popular Chemistry, Hygienic Physiology, and New Descriptive Astronomy. Great pains have been taken to revise and compare the problems, which are fully, and, it is thought, accurately solved. The practical questions, as in the former edition of the Manual, are often not answered in full, yet sufficiently so to furnish a key to the more perfect reply. The use of the text-books is presupposed, and the statements merely supplement, or apply the theories therein contained and explained. Upon many points there may be, and often is, a difference of opinion. On these mooted questions only that view which appeared to the author to have preponderance of argument has been advanced, leaving the subject open for the discussion of other theories.

The former edition of the Manual can still be obtained by those teachers who continue to use the earlier editions of the Sciences, although, with a few exceptions, the problems and questions therein answered are incorporated with those which have been added in the present issue.

DECEMBER, 1888.

ANSWERS

TO THE

PRACTICAL QUESTIONS AND PROBLEMS

IN THE

POPULAR PHYSICS.

36—1. *A rifle-ball* **thrown** *against a board standing on its end will knock it down; the same bullet* **fired** *at the board will pass through it without disturbing its position. Why is this?*

The ball which is thrown has time to impart its motion to the board; the one fired has not.

2. *Why can a boy skate safely over a piece of thin ice, when, if he should pause, it would break under him directly?*

In the latter case there is time for the weight of his body to be communicated to the ice; in the former, there is not.

3. *Why can a cannon-ball be fired through a door standing ajar, without moving it on its hinges?*

Because the cannon-ball is moving so quickly that its motion is not imparted perceptibly to the door.

4. *Why can we drive on the head of a hammer by simply striking the end of the handle?*

This can only be done by a quick, sharp blow, which will drive the wooden handle through the socket before the motion has time to overcome the inertia of the iron head. A slow, steady blow will be imparted to the head, and so fail of the desired effect.

5. Suppose you were on a train of cars moving at the rate of 30 miles per hour; with what force would you be thrown forward if the train were stopped instantly?

With the same velocity which the train had, or 44 feet per second. Your momentum would be your mass multiplied by this velocity.

6. In what line does a stone fall from the mast-head of a vessel in motion?

In a slightly curved line, produced by the two forces—gravity and the forward motion of the vessel.

7. If a ball be dropped from a high tower it will strike the earth a little east of a vertical line. Why is this?

In the daily revolution of the earth on its axis, from west to east, the top of the tower moves faster than the bottom, because it passes through a larger circle. When, therefore, the ball falls, it retains that swifter easterly motion, and so strikes very slightly east of the vertical.

8. It is stated that a suit was once brought by the driver of a light wagon against the owner of a coach for damages caused by a collision. The complaint was that the latter was driving so fast, that when the two carriages struck the driver of the former was thrown forward over the dash-board. Show how his own testimony proved him to have been at fault.

When the light wagon was suddenly stopped, its driver went on with the same speed at which the wagon was moving. That this threw him forward over the dash-board, proves his speed to have been unusual.

9. Suppose a train moving at the rate of 30 miles per hour; on the rear platform is a spring-gun aimed parallel with the track, and in a direction precisely opposite to the motion of the car. Let a ball be discharged with the exact speed of the train, where would it fall?

In a vertical line to the track. The two equal, opposite motions would exactly destroy each other.

10. Suppose a steamer in rapid motion and on its deck a man jumping. Can he jump farther by leaping the way the boat is moving or in the opposite direction?

It will make no difference as long as he jumps on the deck. Should he jump off the boat, then the effect would be different.

11. Could a party play ball on the deck of an ocean steam-ship when moving along at the rate of 20 miles per hour, without making allowance for the motion of the ship?

They could. The ball would have the motion of the ship, and would move with it in whatever direction they might throw it.

37—12. Since "action is equal to reaction," why is it not so dangerous to receive the "kick" of a gun as the force of the bullet?

The kinetic energy varies as the square of the velocity; and the velocity with which the gun moves backward is as much less than that with which the bullet moves forward, as the gun is heavier than the bullet. For this reason a heavy gun will kick much less than a light one.

13. If you were to jump from a carriage in rapid motion, would you leap directly toward the spot on which you wished to alight?

No; because as one jumps from the carriage he has its forward motion, and will go just as far ahead, while leaping, as he would if he had remained in the carriage. He should, therefore, aim a little back of the desired alighting-place.

14. If you wished to shoot a bird in swift flight, would you aim directly at it?

No. The bird will fly forward while the bullet is going to it. One should, therefore, aim a little in advance.

15. At what parts of the earth is the centrifugal force the least?

The poles. The distance from axis to surface is there reduced to zero.

16. What causes the mud to fly from the wheels of a carriage in rapid motion?

The centrifugal force (the momentum of the mud).

17. What proof have we that the earth was once a soft mass?

It is flattened at the poles. This effect is produced upon a ball of soft clay by simply revolving it on a wire axis.

18. On a curve in a railroad, why is one track always higher than the other?

The outer track is raised in order that centrifugal force and gravity, acting together, may combine to keep the average pressure perpendicular to the track.

19. What is the principle of the sling?

The sling is whirled until a strong centrifugal force is generated; the string, the centripetal force, is then released, when the stone flies off at a tangent.

20. The mouth of the Mississippi River is about $2\frac{1}{4}$ miles farther from the center of the earth than its source. What causes its water to thus "run up hill"?

The centrifugal force produced by the rotation of the earth on its axis tends to drive the water from the poles toward the equator. Were the earth to stand still in its daily rotation, the Gulf of Mexico would empty its waters back through the Mississippi to the northern regions.

21. Is it action or reaction that breaks an egg when I strike it against the table?

The reaction of the table.

22. Was the man philosophical who said "it was not the falling so far but the stopping so quick that hurt him"?

He was.

23. If one person runs against another, which receives the greater blow?

Action is equal to reaction; hence the momentum given up by the one is equal to that received by the other.

24. Would it vary the effect if the two persons were running in opposite directions?

The blow would then be the *sum* of both their momenta.

If they were running in the same direction?

The blow would be equal to the *difference* of their momenta.

25. Why can you not fire a rifle-ball around a hill?

Because a single force always produces motion in a straight line.

26. Why does a heavy gun "kick" less than a light one?

See problem 12.

27. A man on the deck of a large steamer draws a small boat toward him. Can you express the ratio of the ship's motion to that of the boat?

The ship moves as much less distance than the boat, as the boat's mass is less than that of the ship.

28. Suppose a string, fastened with a nail at one end, will just support a weight of 25 lbs. at the other. Unfasten it, and let two persons pull upon it in opposite directions. How much can each pull without breaking it?

25 lbs. The second person, in the latter case, can pull as much as the nail did in the former. The *tension* in the string is 25 lbs., and the action of the one person is just balanced by the reaction of the other.

29. Can a man standing on a platform-scale make himself lighter by lifting up on himself?

He can not; because action and reaction are equal and opposite.

30. Why can not a man lift himself by pulling up on his boot-straps?

See last problem.

31. With what momentum would a steam-boat weighing 1,000 tons, and moving with a velocity of 10 feet per second, strike against a sunken rock?

1,000 tons = 2,000,000 lbs. 2,000,000 × 10 = 20,000,000 units of momentum.

32. With what momentum would a train of cars weighing 100 tons, and running 10 miles per hour, strike against an obstacle?

The velocity per second is $14\frac{2}{3}$ feet. 100 tons = 200,000 lbs. The momentum is 200,000 × $14\frac{2}{3}$ = $2,933,333\frac{1}{3}$ units of momentum.

33. What would be the comparative kinetic energy of two hammers, one driven with a velocity of 20 feet per second, and the other 10 feet?

$20^2 = 400$. $10^2 = 100$. 400 : 100 :: 4 : 1.

Hence the kinetic energy of the first, or its ability to accomplish work, will be four times that of the second. This principle is of great importance in all cases where percussion is concerned. The highest velocity attainable is to be sought.

34. If a 100 horse-power engine can propel a steamer 5 miles per hour, will one of 200 horse-power double its speed?

By no means. Resistance is proportional to v^2. (See *Popular Physics*, p. 65.) To double the velocity would require over 400 horse-power.

35. Why are ships becalmed at sea sometimes floated by strong currents into dangerous localities without the knowledge of the crew?

As there are no fixed objects with which to compare their motion, the officers are not sensible of any movement, and so are drifted far out of their course.

38—*36. A man in a wagon holds a 50-lb. weight in his hand. Suddenly the wagon falls over a precipice. Will he, while dropping, bear the strain of the weight?*

No. While on solid ground, his hand resisted the tendency of the weight to fall toward the earth's center of gravity; but all are now descending freely under the influence of gravity, and he no longer feels the pressure.

37. Why are we not sensible of the rapid motion of the earth?

Because all the objects around us are moving in the same direction with the earth, and there is nothing at hand with which to compare.

38. A feather is dropped from a balloon which is immersed in and swept along by a swift current of air. Will the feather be blown away, or will it appear to a person in the balloon to drop directly down?

It will seem to drop directly downward, as if in a dead calm. Its fall is vertical, however, only as regards the balloon, and not as regards the earth.

(See Stewart's *Physics*, p. 18.)

39. Suppose a bomb-shell, flying through the air at the rate of 500 feet per second, explodes into two parts of equal weight, driving one half forward in the same direction as before, but with double its former velocity. What would become of the other half?

One half will go forward with a double velocity (= 1,000 feet per sec.), and the other half will be checked and will fall directly to the ground.

(See Stewart's *Physics*, p. 37.)

40. Which would have the greater penetrating power, a small cannon-ball with a high velocity, or a large one with a low velocity?

The former would penetrate, while the latter would have the greater momentum.

41. There is a story told of a man who erected a huge pair of bellows in the stern of his pleasure-boat, that he might always have a fair wind. On trial, the plan failed. In which direction should he have turned the bellows?

In the manner adopted at first, of turning the nozzle toward the sails, the action of the wind against the sails and the reaction of the bellows against the boat just balanced each other. If the man had turned the nozzle backward, he could have saved the reaction of the bellows to move the boat. This would, however, have been a costly and bungling mode of navigation.

42. If a man and a boy were riding in a wagon, and, on coming to the foot of a hill, the man should take up the boy in his arms, would that help the horse?

No change would be produced in the weight of the entire establishment drawn by the horse, as no readjustment of the load would modify the attraction of gravity which produces the weight. Also, action = reaction; so the man would press down on the wagon an amount equal to the weight of the boy.

43. If we whirl a pail of water swiftly around on its own axis, why will the water tend to leave the center of the pail?

The centrifugal force is compounded with the force of gravity, and at each point of the surface the water level is at right angles to their resultant. The centrifugal force increases with distance from the axis, hence the water surface becomes concave.

44. Why will the foam collect at the hollow in the center?

The foam, being lighter than the water, has less momentum, in proportion to its volume, and is forced back by the heavier particles.

45. If two cannon-balls, one weighing 8 lbs. and the other 2 lbs., be fired with the same velocity, which will go the farther?

The former has much less surface in proportion to its weight. It will therefore go much farther against the resistance of the air.

46. Resolve the force of the wind which turns a common windmill, and show how one part acts to push the wheel against its support, and one to turn it around.

This case is exactly like that of the action of the wind against the sail of a ship, as shown in the text on p. 29.

47. When an animal is jumping or falling, can any exertion made in mid-air change the motion of its center of gravity?

The center of gravity falls steadily 16.08 feet, whatever other force may act on the body.

(See Second Law of Motion.)

48. If one is riding rapidly, in which direction will he be thrown when the horse is suddenly stopped?

In the same direction in which he is going. He has the motion of the carriage, and his momentum carries him forward.

49. When standing in a boat, why, as it starts, are we thrown backward?

Because our bodies tend to remain stationary, while the boat carries our feet forward.

50. When carrying a cup of tea, if we move or stop quickly, why is the liquid liable to spill?

The momentum of the tea tends to keep it still or in motion, as the case may be. If we move the cup quickly, the motion is not imparted to the liquid soon enough to overcome this momentum. When, therefore, we start, the tea spills out backward; or, when we stop, it spills out forward. We understand this if we can tell why a cup of tea is more liable to spill than one of sugar.

51. Why, when closely pursued, can we escape by dodging?

We turn sharply. Our pursuer, ignorant of our design, can not overcome his momentum so as to turn as quickly, and hence is carried past.

52. Why is a carriage or sleigh, when sharply turning a corner, liable to tip over?

Because its momentum tends to carry it directly forward.

53. Why, if you place a card on your finger, and on top of it a cent, can you snap the card from under the cent without knocking the latter off your finger?

Because the friction between the card and the cent is so slight that, by a quick snap, you can give motion to the former without affecting the latter enough to make it fall off.

54. Why is a "running jump" longer than a "standing jump"?

This is an example under the first law of motion. The momentum of the person when running ($m \times v$) is added to the force with which he finally springs from the ground for the jump.

55. Why, after the sails of a vessel are furled, does it still continue to move? and why, after the sails are spread, does it require some time to get it under full headway?

This illustrates the tendency of matter to continue in its present state, whether of rest or of motion. For the former part of the question, apply the first law of motion, and for the latter, the second paragraph on p. 21 of the *Physics*. If, on starting with a heavy load, the horses leap suddenly forward, they will break the harness; but, by a steady, constantly-increased draught, they will communicate motion to the mass.

56. Why can a tallow candle be fired through a board?

Because of its high velocity. Motion can not be communicated at once to the entire mass of the board, hence this yields at the place where pressure is suddenly applied.

COHESION.

48—1. Why can we not weld a piece of copper to one of iron?

Cohesion acts most readily between molecules of the same kind.

2. Why is a bar of iron stronger than one of wood?

All we can say is that there is more cohesion between its molecules. The wood, moreover, is perforated with minute hollow tubes, so that its molecules can not be so compactly massed together as those of the iron.

3. Why may a piece of iron, when perfectly welded, be stronger than before it was broken?

By the hammering, more particles are brought within the range of cohesion.

4. Why do drops of different liquids vary in size?

Because they vary in cohesive force.

5. Why, when you drop medicine, will the last few drops contained in the bottle be of a larger size than the others?

The pressure of the liquid in the bottle is less, and therefore they form more slowly.

6. Why are drops larger if you drop them slowly?

There is more time for the adhesive force of the bottle to act on the liquid, and so a larger drop can be gathered.

7. Why, if you melt scraps of zinc, will they form a solid mass when cooled?

The heat overcomes, in part, the attraction of cohesion, so that the particles flow freely on each other. They now all come within the range of cohesion, so that when the metal cools they are held by that force in a solid mass.

8. In what liquids is the force of cohesion greatest?

Mercury, molasses, etc.

9. Name some solids that will volatilize without melting.

Arsenic, camphor.

10. Why can glass be welded?

Because, like iron, it becomes viscous before melting.

11. Name some substances that can not be welded. Why not?

Wood can not be welded, nor can lead or bismuth. They can not be made to assume the viscous condition.

12. What liquids would you select for showing surface tension?

Solution of soap in water is the most convenient. The difference in tension between films of different kinds of liquid is well shown by carefully dropping oil of coriander or oil of cinnamon, or minute fragments of clean camphor on the surface of perfectly clean water.

ADHESION.

54—1. *Why does cloth shrink when wet?*

By adhesion the water is drawn into the pores of the cloth. The fibers are thus expanded sidewise and shortened lengthwise. The cloth *"fulls up"* or thickens while it shortens and narrows (*shrinks*) in the process.

2. *Why do sailors at a boat-race wet the sails?*

The pores being full and expanded make the sails more compact. They will, therefore, hold the wind better.

3. *Why does not writing-paper blot?*

Because the pores are filled with sizing. (See *Popular Chemistry*, p. 216.)

4. *Why does paint tend to prevent wood from shrinking?*

Because it fills the pores of the wood at its surface.

5. *What is the shape of the surface of a glass of water and one of mercury?*

Ordinarily the former is concave and the latter convex.

6. *Why can we not dry a towel perfectly by wringing?*

Because of the strength of the force of adhesion, by which the water is held in the pores of the cloth.

7. *Why will not water run through a fine sieve when the wires have been greased?*

Because of reversed capillarity between oil and water.

8. *Why will camphor dissolve easily in alcohol and not in water?*

Because there is a strong adhesion between the alcohol and camphor, and but little between the water and camphor.

9. *Why will mercury rise in zinc tubes as water does in glass tubes?*

Because of the strong adhesion between zinc and mercury.

10. Why will ink spilled on the edge of a book extend farther inside than if spilled on the side of the leaves?

Because the sensible pores of the paper are short, being only the thickness of a leaf, while the spaces between the leaves are longer and continuous.

11. If you should happen to spill some ink on the edge of your book, ought you to press the leaves together?

Yes; to make it as nearly solid as possible, until blotting paper can be applied to remove what has not soaked into the book.

12. Why can you not mix oil and water?

Because there is little adhesion between them.

13. Why will water wet your hand while mercury will not?

Because in the former case there is strong adhesion, in the latter but little.

14. Why is a tub or pail liable to fall to pieces if not filled with water or kept in the cellar?

Because the moisture dries out of the pores, and the wood shrinks so as to let the hoops fall off.

15. Name instances where the attraction of adhesion is stronger than that of cohesion.

Wood fastened by glue will often split before the glue will yield. Paper stuck with paste, and bricks with mortar, are also examples.

16. Why does the water in Fig. 18 stand higher inside of the tube than next the glass on the outside?

There is the influence of a larger surface of glass in proportion to the quantity of water to be lifted.

17. Why will clothes-lines tighten and sometimes break during a shower?

The rope absorbs water, and expands transversely. This shortens it with so much force as often to break it. The shrinking of new cloth when wet illustrates the same principle.

18. In casting large cannon, the gun is cooled by a stream of cold water. Why?

The object of this is to cause the iron to cool more quickly, and so not give the molecules time to arrange themselves in crystals.

19. Why does paint adhere to wood? Chalk to the blackboard?

These are illustrations of the force of adhesion.

20. Why does a towel dry one's face after washing?

The sensible pores of the cloth absorb the water from the face by adhesion.

21. Why will a greased needle float on water?

The grease prevents the needle from being wetted, and the toughness of the surface film of water is sufficient to withstand the weight of the needle.

22. Why is the point of a pen slit?

So that we may widen at will the surface of contact between the ink and the paper. The ink is prevented from descending rapidly, when the slit is not open, by the grip of its surface film.

23. Why is a thin layer of glue stronger than a thick one?

The adhesion between the glue and the wood is stronger than the cohesion between the particles of glue; hence the thinner the layer of glue the fewer the particles acted upon only by the latter or weaker force.

GRAVITATION.

73—1. When an apple falls to the ground, how much does the earth rise to meet it?

The earth falls as much less distance than the apple, as its mass is greater.

2. Will a body weigh more in a valley than on a mountain?

It will, because the distance to the earth's center is less.

3. Will a pound weight fall more slowly than a two-pound weight?

They will both fall in the same time, except the slight difference which is caused by the resistance of the air. Galileo propounded this view, and proved it, in the presence of witnesses, by letting unequal weights fall from the leaning tower of Pisa.

4. How deep is a well, if it takes three seconds for a stone to fall to the bottom of it?

$$S = \tfrac{1}{2}gt^2$$
$$S = 16 \times 3^2 = 144 \text{ feet.}$$

5. Is the center of gravity always within a body—as, for example, a pair of tongs?

No. It may be entirely outside, and is usually so for a pair of tongs.

6. In a ball of equal density throughout, where is the center of gravity?

At the center of the ball.

7. Why does a ball roll down hill?

Because the line of direction falls without the small base of the ball.

8. Why is it easier to roll a round body than a square one?

Because the base of the ball is so much smaller, and therefore the center of gravity need not be raised to bring the line of direction without.

9. Why is it easier to tip over a load of hay than one of stone?

Because the center of gravity in a load of hay is very high, and in a load of stone very low. Therefore the center of gravity in the former need not be raised much to bring the line of direction without the base, while in the latter it must be.

10. Why is a pyramid the stablest of structures?

Because the base is so broad and the center of gravity so low. The center of gravity must therefore be lifted very high before the line of direction will fall without the base.

11. When a hammer is thrown, on which end does it most often strike?

The heavier end.

12. Why does a rope-walker carry a heavy balancing-pole?

Because in this way he can easily shift his center of gravity.

13. What would become of a ball if dropped into a hole bored through the center of the earth?

If we assume the earth to be at rest, the ball will move with diminishing acceleration, but increasing speed, to the center. The momentum thus acquired would carry it an equal distance beyond, if there be no resistances, and the acceleration being now negative, the ball will be brought momentarily to rest at the surface on the opposite side. It will then fall back past the center, and continue thus oscillating forever. If we assume the earth to be rotating, the ball will sink from fast-moving toward slow-moving parts, and strike against the side of the hole. Friction will soon bring it to rest at the earth's center.

14. Would a clock lose or gain time if carried to the top of a mountain?

It would lose time, because the force of gravity would be lessened. At the North Pole it would gain time, because there the force of gravity would be increased.

15. In the winter, would you raise or lower the pendulum-bob of your clock?

I would lower it, since the cold of winter shortens the pendulum, and this movement of the bob would counteract that change.

16. Why is the pendulum-bob generally made flat?
To decrease the friction of the air.

17. What beats off the time in a watch?
The vibration of the balance-wheel.

18. Is solved in the book.

19. What should be the length of a pendulum at New York to vibrate half-seconds?

(1 sec.)^2 : ($\frac{1}{2}$ sec.)^2 :: 39.1 in. : x = 9.7 + inches.

To vibrate quarter-seconds?

(1 sec.)^2 : ($\frac{1}{4}$ sec.)^2 :: 39.1 in. : x = 2.4 + inches.

To vibrate hours?

(1 sec.)^2 : (3600 sec.)^2 :: 39.1 in. : x = 7997.7 miles.*

20. What is the proportionate time of vibration of two pendulums, 16 and 64 inches long, respectively?

According to the 2d law of pendulums,
Time of vib. of 1st : Time of vib. of 2d :: $\sqrt{16}$: $\sqrt{64}$ :: 4 : 8 :: 1 : 2.

21. Why, when you are standing erect against a wall, and a piece of money is placed between your feet, can you not stoop forward and pick it up?

By leaning forward you bring the center of gravity in front of your feet, and, as on account of the wall, you can not throw any part of your body back to preserve the balance, you fall forward.

22. If a tower were 198 feet high, with what velocity would a stone, dropped from the summit, strike the ground?

v^2 = 2gh   (See p. 64, foot-note.)
v^2 = 64 × 198
v = 112.5 feet.

* Nearly the diameter of the earth.

23. *A body falls in 5 seconds; with what velocity does it strike the ground?*

$v = 32t$. $v = 32 \times 5$. $v = 160$ feet.

74—24. *How far will a body fall in 10 seconds?*

$s = 16t^2$. $s = 16 \times 10^2 = 1600$ feet.

With what velocity will it strike the ground?

$v = 32t$. $v = 32 \times 10 = 320$ feet.

25. *A body is thrown upward with a velocity of 192 feet the first second; to what height will it rise?*

Equation (1), $v = 32t$. $192 = 32t$. $t = 6$ sec.
" (2), $s = 16t^2$. $s = 16 \times 6^2 = 576$ feet.

26. *A ball is shot upward with a velocity of 256 feet; to what height will it rise? How long will it continue to ascend?*

Using equations (1) and (2), as in the last problem, we have

$t = 8$ sec.
$s = 1024$ feet.

28. *Are any two plumb-lines parallel?*

They are not, since they point to the earth's center of gravity. No two spokes of a wheel can be parallel.

29. *A stone let fall from a bridge strikes the water in three seconds. What is the height?*

$s = 16t^2$. $s = 16 \times 3^2 = 144$ feet.

30. *A stone falls from a church steeple in 4 seconds. What is the height?*

$s = 16t^2$. $s = 16 \times 4^2 = 256$ feet.

31. *How far would a body fall the first second at a height of 12,000 miles above the earth's surface?*

$(16,000 \text{ mi.})^2 : (4000 \text{ mi.})^2 :: 16 \text{ feet} : x = 1$ foot.

32. *A body at the surface of the earth weighs 100 tons; what would be its weight 1,000 miles above?*

$(5000 \text{ mi.})^2 : (4000 \text{ mi.})^2 :: 100 \text{ tons} : x = 64$ tons.

33. A boy wishing to find the height of a steeple lets fly an arrow that just reaches the top, and then falls to the ground. It is in the air 6 seconds. Required the height.

$$s = 16t^2. \quad s = 16 \times 3^2 = 144 \text{ feet.}$$

34. An object let fall from a balloon reaches the ground in 10 seconds. Required the distance.

$$s = 16 \times 10^2 = 1600 \text{ ft.}$$

35. In what time will a pendulum 40 feet long make a vibration?

According to the 2d law of pendulums, and taking the length of a seconds pendulum as 39 in., we have:

$$1 \text{ sec.} : x :: \sqrt{39} : \sqrt{40 \times 12 \text{ in.}}$$

$$x = \sqrt{\frac{480}{39}}$$

$$x = 3.5 + \text{sec.}$$

36. Two bodies in space are 12 miles apart. They weigh 100 and 200 lbs. respectively. If they should fall together by force of their mutual attraction, what portion of the distance would be passed over by each body?

The distance passed over by the two bodies is inversely as their mass; hence one moves 8 miles and the other 4 miles.

37. If a body weighs 2,000 lbs. upon the surface of the earth, what would it weigh 2,000 miles above?

$$(6000 \text{ mi.})^2 : (4000 \text{ mi.})^2 :: 2000 \text{ lbs.} : x = 888\tfrac{8}{9} \text{ lbs.}$$

How much 500 miles above?

$$(4500 \text{ mi.})^2 : (4000 \text{ mi.})^2 :: 2000 \text{ lbs.} : x = 1580 + \text{lbs.}$$

38. At what distance above the surface of the earth will a body fall, the first second, $21\tfrac{1}{3}$ inches?

A body falls 16 feet* (192 inches) at the surface of the earth. $21\tfrac{1}{3}$ inches are $\tfrac{1}{9}$ of 192 inches. Now, as the attraction is inversely as the square of the distance, the distance must be

---

* According to the best authorities the distance is more nearly $16\tfrac{1}{12}$ feet.

$\sqrt{9}$, or 3 times that at the surface. Hence, the body must be 12,000 miles from the center, or 8,000 miles from the surface of the earth. The problem may be solved directly by proportion, thus:

$$x^2 : 4000^2 :: 192 \text{ inches} : 21\tfrac{1}{3} \text{ inches.}$$
$$x = 12000 \text{ miles (distance from the center).}$$
$$12000 \text{ miles} - 4000 \text{ miles} = 8000 \text{ miles.}$$

39. How far will a body fall in 8 seconds? 1,024 feet.—In the 8th second? 240 feet.—In 10 seconds? 1,600 feet.—In the 30th second? 944 feet.

40. How long would it take for a pendulum one mile in length to make a vibration?

According to the second law of pendulums (*Physics*, p. 69),

$$1 \text{ sec.} : x :: \sqrt{39} : \sqrt{5280 \times 12 \text{ in.}}$$
$$x = 40 + \text{sec.}$$

41. What would be the time of vibration of a pendulum 64 meters long?

$$(1 \text{ sec.})^2 : x^2 :: 1 \text{ meter (nearly)} : 64 \text{ meters.}$$
$$x = 8 \text{ seconds (nearly).}$$

42. A ball is dropped from a height of 64 feet. At the same moment a second ball is thrown upward with sufficient velocity to reach the same point. Where will the two balls pass each other?

At the end of one second. The first ball would fall 64 feet in 2 seconds; the second would rise for 2 seconds, and they would pass in 1 second, 48 feet above the ground.

43. Explain the following fact: A straight stick loaded with lead at one end can be more easily balanced vertically on the finger when the loaded end is upward than when it is downward.

When the loaded end is upward a slighter motion is needed to bring the line of direction within the base. The principle is similar to that of the balancing-pole of the gymnast.

44. *If a body weighing 1 lb. on the earth were carried to the sun, it would weigh 27 lbs. How much would it attract the sun? Ans.* **27** lbs.

75—45. *Why does watery vapor float and rain fall?*

Perfect vapor, which is quite invisible, is lighter than air, and is diffused through it. When condensed into minute droplets forming clouds, these are prevented from falling fast because of the great amount of surface, in proportion to their weight, exposed to the resistance of the air.

46. *If a body weighs 10 kilos. on the surface of the earth, what will it weigh 1,000 km. above?*

$$x : 10 \text{ kilos.} :: (6{,}366*)^2 : (7{.}366)^2$$
$$x = 7.5 \text{ kilograms.}$$

47. *A body is thrown vertically upward with a velocity of 100 meters. How long before it will return to its original position? Ans.* **20.4** *seconds.*

48. *How much time will be required for a body to fall a distance of 2,000 meters?*

$$\text{Equation (6)} \quad s = \tfrac{1}{2}gt^2. \quad 2{,}000 = \frac{9.8}{2}t^2.$$
$$\therefore t = 20.2 \text{ seconds.}$$

49. *What would be the time of vibration of a pendulum 39.1 inches long at the surface of the moon, where the acceleration of gravity is only 4.8 ft.?*

$$t : t' :: \frac{1}{\sqrt{g}} : \frac{1}{\sqrt{g'}} \quad \text{(see 3d Law of Pendulum, p. 69).}$$
$$1 : t' :: \frac{1}{\sqrt{32}} : \frac{1}{\sqrt{4.8}}$$
$$t' = 2.58 \text{ seconds.}$$

50. *What would be the time of vibration for the same pendulum at the surface of the sun, where the accel-*

---

* The radius, or semi-diameter of the earth, is given by French astronomers at 6,366 km.

eration of gravity is 27 times what it is at the earth's surface?

$$1 : t' :: \frac{1}{\sqrt{32}} : \frac{1}{\sqrt{27 \times 32}}$$

$t' = .19 + $ second.

51. How many vibrations per minute would be made at the surface of the moon by a pendulum 40 ft. long?

First find the time of a single vibration.

$$1 : t :: \sqrt{\frac{39.1}{32}} : \sqrt{\frac{40 \times 12}{4.8}}$$

$t = 9 + $ seconds.

Hence, in a minute, the number of vibrations will be not quite 7.

52. A pendulum vibrates 200 times in 15 minutes. What is its length?

$\frac{15 \times 60}{200} = 4\frac{1}{2}$ seconds, the time of a single vibration.

$$1 : 4\frac{1}{2} :: \sqrt{39.1} : \sqrt{x}$$

$x = 791.8$ inches, or 66 feet nearly.

53. For a certain clock in New York the pendulum was made 500 lbs. in weight. What was the object in making it so heavy?

To secure regularity of motion by means of the large mass, so that variations in resistance may be avoided as nearly as possible.

54. Pendulums are often supported by knife-edges of steel resting on plates of agate. Why?

Because the friction between steel and agate is less than if any other substances are used. It is desirable to avoid friction as completely as possible.

55. The acceleration of gravity at the equator is 32.088 ft.; at the pole, 32.253 ft. If a pendulum vibrates 3,600 times an hour at the equator, how many times an hour will it vibrate at the pole?

The number of vibrations per hour varies inversely as the time of vibration of the pendulum. For t in the formula, therefore, we may substitute the reciprocal of the number of vibrations per hour.

$$\frac{1}{3600} : \frac{1}{x} :: \frac{1}{\sqrt{32.088}} : \frac{1}{\sqrt{32.253}}$$
$$x = 3{,}609.36 \text{ times.}$$

THE MECHANICAL POWERS.

94—1. *Describe the rudder of a boat as a lever.*

The water is the F, the boat the W, and the hand the P. As the W is between the F and the P, it is a lever of the second class. By similar reasoning it is easy to analyze the remaining cases, a door, a door-latch, etc.

95—2. *Show the change that occurs from the second to the third class of levers, when you take hold of a ladder at one end and raise it against a building.*

At first the ground is the F at one end, the hand the P at the other, and the ladder the W hanging between; hence this is a lever of the second class. After a little, the F remaining the same, the P is applied at one end, near the F, and the ladder is the W hanging at the other; hence this is now a lever of the third class.

3. Why is a pinch from the tongs near the hinge more severe than one near the end?

Because in the former case the tongs are a lever of the first class—in the latter, of the third. In the first class there is a gain of power, in the third a loss.

4. Two persons are carrying a weight of 250 lbs., hanging between them from a pole 10 feet in length. Where should it be suspended so that one will lift only 50 lbs.?

One lifts 50 lbs.; the other 200 lbs. The proportionate length of the arms of the lever should be the same as the proportionate weights—*i.e.*, 1 to 4. $10 \div 5 = 2$, the unit of measure. Hence one arm is 2 feet long and the other 8 feet long. PROOF.—$50 \times 8 = 200 \times 2$. This is the substance also of the equation $P \times Pd = W \times Wd$.

5. In a lever of the first class, 6 feet long, where should the F be placed so that a P of 1 lb. will balance a W of 23 lbs.?

6 feet = 72 inches. $72 \div 24 = 3$, the unit of distance. The W must be placed 3 in. and the P 69 in. from the F. PROOF.— $23 \times 3 = 1 \times 69$ (Prob. 4).

6. What P would be required to lift a barrel of pork with a windlass whose axle is one foot in diameter and handle 3 ft. long?

P : W : rad. of axle :: rad. of wheel.
x : 200 lbs. :: $\frac{1}{2}$ ft. : 3 ft.
$x = 33\frac{1}{3}$ lbs.

7. What sized axle, with a wheel 6 feet in diameter, would be required to balance a W of 1 ton by a P of 100 lbs.?

P : W :: diameter of axle : diameter of wheel.
100 lbs. : 2,000 lbs. :: x : 6 ft.
$x = \frac{3}{10}$ ft. = the diameter.

8. What number of movable pulleys would be required to lift a W of 200 lbs. with a P of 25 lbs.?

$W = P \times$ twice the number of movable pulleys;
hence $\frac{W}{P} = $ twice the number of movable pulleys.
$200 \div 25 = 8$. $8 \div 2 = 4 =$ the number required.

9. How many lbs. could be lifted with a system of 4 movable pulleys, and one fixed pulley to change the direction of the force, by a P of 100 lbs.?

$W = P \times$ twice the number of movable pulleys.
100 lbs. $\times (4 \times 2) = 800$ lbs. = the W.

10. *What weight could be lifted with a single horse power (33,000 lbs. one foot high per minute) acting on a system of pulleys shown in Fig. 62?*

W = 33,000 × 2 × 2 × 2 × 2 = 528,000 lbs.

11. *What distance should there be between the threads of a screw, that a P of 25 lbs., acting on a handle 3 ft. long, may lift 1 ton weight?*

P : W :: Interval : Circumference.
25 lbs. : 2,000 lbs. :: x : 72 in. × 3.1416.
x = 2.83 − in.

12. *How high could a P of 12 lbs., moving 16 ft. along an inclined plane, lift a W of 96 lbs.?*

P : W :: height : length.
12 lbs. : 96 lbs. :: x : 16 ft.
x = 2 ft.

13. *I wish to roll a barrel of flour into a wagon, the box of which is 4 ft. from the ground. I can lift but 24 lbs. How long a plank should I get?*

P : W :: height : length.
24 lbs. : 196 lbs. :: 4 ft. : x = $32\frac{2}{3}$ ft.

14. *What W can be lifted with a P of 100 lbs. acting on a screw having threads 1 in. apart, and a handle 4 ft. long?*

P : W :: Interval : Circumference.
100 : x :: 1 : 4 × 12 × 3.1416
x = 15,079.68.

15. *What is the object of the balls often cast on the ends of the handle of the screw used in presses for copying letters?*

By their momentum they make the motion more uniform and continuous.

16. *In a steelyard 2 ft. long, the distance from the weight-hook to the fulcrum-hook is 2 in. How heavy a body can be weighed with a 1 lb. weight?*

24 in. − 2 in. = 22 in.   1 lb. × 22 = 22 lbs. = P.
22 lbs. ÷ 2 = 11 lbs. = W.

17. Describe the change from the 1st to the 3d class of levers, in the different ways of using a spade.

When digging, the ground at the back of the spade is the F; the ground lifted is the W; and the hand at the other end is the P. As the W is at one end, P at the other, and the F between, this is a lever of the 1st class. When throwing dirt, the left hand at one end of the spade is the F; the dirt at the other end is the W, and the right hand between the two is the P. As the P is between the F and the W, this is a lever of the 3d class.

18. Why are not blacksmiths' tongs and fire tongs constructed on the same principle?

The former are of the 1st class, as power is required: the latter of the 3d class, as rapidity only is necessary.

19. In a lever of the 3d class, what W will a P of 50 lbs. balance, if one arm is 12 ft. and the other 3 ft. long?

$$P : W :: Wd : Pd.$$
$$50 \text{ lbs.} : x :: 12 \text{ ft.} : 3 \text{ ft.}$$
$$x = 12\tfrac{1}{2} \text{ lbs.}$$

96—20. In a lever of the 2d class, what W will a P of 50 lbs. balance, with a lever 12 feet long and W 3 feet from the F?

$$50 \text{ lbs.} : x :: 3 \text{ ft.} : 12 \text{ ft.}$$
$$x = 200 \text{ lbs.}$$

21. In a lever of the 1st class, what W will a P of 50 lbs. balance, with a lever 12 ft. long and the F 3 ft. from the W?

$$50 \text{ lbs.} : x :: 3 \text{ ft.} : 9 \text{ ft.}$$
$$x = 150 \text{ lbs.}$$

22. In a wheel and axle, the P = 40 lbs., W = 360 lbs., diameter of axle = 8 in. Required the circumference of the wheel.

$$P : W :: \text{diameter of axle} : \text{diam. of wheel.}$$
40 lbs. : 360 lbs. :: 8 in. : x = 72 in. = 6 ft., the diameter of wheel.
6 ft. × 3.1416 = 18.85 ft., the circumference of the wheel.

23. *Suppose in a wheel and axle the $P = 20$ lbs., the $W = 240$ lbs., and the diameter of wheel $= 4$ ft. Required the circumference of the axle.*

$$20 \text{ lbs.} : 240 \text{ lbs.} :: x : 48 \text{ in.}$$
$$x = 4 \text{ in. (diameter of axle).}$$
$$4 \text{ in.} \times 3.1416 = 12.56 \text{ in. (circumference).}$$

24. *Required, in a wheel and axle, the diameter of the wheel, the diameter of the axle being 10 inches, $P = 100$ lbs. and $W = 1$ ton.*

$$100 \text{ lbs.} : 2{,}000 \text{ lbs.} :: 10 \text{ in.} : x = 200 \text{ in.} = 16\tfrac{2}{3} \text{ ft.}$$

25. *Why is the rim of a fly-wheel made so heavy?*

The largest momentum possible is desired. The velocity of a particle is proportional to its radius in rotation. Hence the largest part of the mass of the wheel is fixed at the rim.

26. *Describe the hammer, when used in drawing a nail, as a bent lever, i.e., one in which the bar is not straight.*

If a lever is bent, or if, when it is straight, the bar is not at right angles to the lines of action of the P and the W, it is necessary to distinguish between the arms of a lever and the arms of the P and the W, regarded as forces which have moments around the F. In the latter sense, the arms are the perpendiculars, dropped from the F to the lines of action of the P and the W.

27. *Describe the four levers shown in Fig. 46, when both the load of hay and the weight are considered, respectively, as the W and the P.*

This is so fully answered in the text that no further explanation seems necessary. The pupil should be required to assume values for the W and for each of the lever arms, and compute the weight of the wagon and hay together. Call his attention to the fact that half the weight of the wagon and hay is transmitted at the point P, and the other half at P'; also that the vertical rod at the lift serves only as a connector, and not as a lever.

HYDROSTATICS.

119—1. Why can housekeepers test the strength of lye, by trying whether or not an egg will float on it?

The potash dissolved in the water to form lye increases the density of the liquid. When enough has been dissolved to make its specific gravity greater than that of the egg, the egg will float. This becomes, therefore, a simple but rough means of testing the amount of potash contained in the lye.

2. How much water will it take to make a gallon of strong brine?

A gallon. The salt does not increase the volume of the liquid.

3. Why ought a fat man to swim more easily than a lean one?

Because muscles and bones are heavier than fat. The specific gravity of a fat man is, therefore, less than that of a lean one.

6. If we let bubbles of air pass up through a jar of water, why will they become larger as they ascend?

The pressure of the water is less as they near the top, and so they expand.

7. What is the pressure on a canal lock-gate 14 feet high and 10 feet wide, when the lock is full of water?

$14 \times 10 \times 7 \times 1{,}000$ oz. $= 980{,}000$ oz. $= 61{,}250$ lbs.

8. Will a pail of water weigh any more with a live fish in it than without?

If the pail were full before the fish was put in, then it will make no difference, since the fish will displace its own weight of water, which will run over. If the pail is only partially filled, then, though the fish is upheld by the buoyancy of the water, since action is equal to reaction, it adds its own weight to that of the water.

9. *If the water filtering down through a rock should collect in a crevice an inch square and 250 feet high, opening at the bottom into a closed fissure having 20 square feet of surface, what would be the total pressure tending to burst the rock?*

Neglecting the diameter of the fissure, the pressure is the same on every square inch of the twenty square feet of surface.

$$\frac{250 \times 1{,}000 \text{ oz.} \times 20 \times 144}{144} = 312{,}500 \text{ lbs.}$$

10. *Why can stones in water be moved so much more easily than on land?*

Because the water buoys up nearly one half of their weight.

11. *Why is it so difficult to wade in the water where there is any current?*

Because we have to move not only the weight of our own bodies, but also the water. The kinetic energy of this is proportional to the mass displaced, and to the square of its velocity.

12. *Why is a mill-dam or a canal embankment made small at the top and large at the bottom?*

Because the pressure of the water increases with the depth.

13. *In digging canals, ought the engineer to take into consideration the curvature of the earth?*

There is no necessity to do so. A water level is in practice assumed to be horizontal. In geodetic surveys, like that of the coast line of a country, allowance has to be made for the curvature of the earth. Station points twenty miles apart, or more, are taken, between which the earth's curvature is readily calculable and perceptible.

14. *Why does the bubble of air in a spirit-level move as the instrument is turned?*

Because the air is lighter than the alcohol, and rises constantly to the highest point. For this reason, also, the tube is curved so as to be convex at the center.

15. Can a swimmer tread on pieces of glass at the bottom of the water with less danger than on land?

Yes. But he would still find it unadvisable to try the experiment.

16. Will a vessel displace more water in a fresh river than in the ocean?

In the fresh river, because the specific gravity, and hence the buoyancy, of fresh water is less.

17. Will iron sink in mercury?

No. It will float, like a cork on water.

18. The water in the reservoir in New York is about 80 feet above the fountain in the City Hall Park. What is the pressure on a single inch of the pipe at the latter point?

$$(1{,}000 \text{ oz.} \times 80) \div 144 = 34.7 \text{ lbs.}$$

19. Why does cream rise on milk?

Because it is lighter than the milk.

20. There is a story told of a Chinese boy who accidentally dropped his ball into a deep hole, where he could not reach it. He filled the hole with water, but the ball would not quite float. He finally bethought himself of a lucky expedient, which was successful. Can you guess it?

He put salt in the water.

21. Which has the greater buoyant force, oil or water?

Water, because its density is greater.

22. What is the weight of 4 cu. ft. of cork?

$1{,}000$ oz. = the weight of 1 cu. ft. of water.
$.240$ = the spec. grav. of cork.
———
240 oz. = the weight of 1 cu. ft. of cork.
4
———
960 oz. = the weight of 4 cu. ft. of cork,
= 60 lbs.

23. How many oz. of iron will a cubic foot of cork float in water?

1,000 oz. = weight of a cubic foot of water.
.240   = spec. grav. of cork.
───────
240   = weight of a cubic foot of cork.

1,000 oz. − 240 oz. = 760 oz., the buoyant force of a cubic foot.

24. What is the specific gravity of a body whose weight in air is 30 grs. and in water 20 grs.?

30 grs. − 20 grs. = 10 grs.
30 grs. ÷ 10 grs. = 3.

The body is three times as heavy as water.

25. Which is heavier, a pail of fresh-water or one of salt-water?

A pail of salt-water is as much heavier than one of fresh-water as the weight of the salt added to make the brine.

26. The weights of a piece of syenite-rock in air and in water were 3941.8 grs. and 2607.5 grs. Find its spec. grav.—Ans. 2.954.

27. A specimen of green sapphire from Siam weighed in air 21.45 grs., and in water 16.33 grs. Required its spec. grav.—Ans. 4.189.

28. A specimen of granite weighs in air 534.8 grs., and in water 334.6 grs. What is the spec. grav.?—Ans. 2.671.

29. What is the volume of a ton of iron?

1,000 oz. = weight of 1 cu. ft. of water
7.8   = spec. grav. of iron.
───────
7,800 oz. = weight of a cu. ft. of iron.

32,000 oz. (a ton of iron) ÷ 7,800 (weight of a cu. ft.) = $4\frac{4}{15}$ cu. ft.

ANSWERS TO PRACTICAL QUESTIONS

A ton of gold?

$$1{,}000 \text{ oz.} = \text{weight of a cu. ft. of water.}$$
$$19.34 = \text{spec. grav. of gold.}$$
$$\overline{19{,}340 \text{ oz.}}\text{*} = \text{weight of a cu. ft. of gold.}$$
$$32{,}000 \text{ oz.*} \div 19{,}340 \text{ oz.} = 1.6, \text{ the no. of cu. ft.}$$

A ton of copper?

$$1{,}000 \text{ oz.} \times 8.9 = 8{,}900 \text{ oz.}$$
$$32{,}000 \text{ oz.} \div 8{,}900 \text{ oz.} = 3.6 \text{ (nearly) the no. of cu. ft.}$$

30. What is the weight of a cube of gold 4 feet on each side?

$$4^3 = 64, \text{ the no. of cu. ft.}$$
$$19{,}340 \text{ oz.*} \text{ (no of oz. in 1 cu. ft.)} \times 64 = 77{,}360 \text{ lbs.}$$

31. A cistern is 12 ft. long, 6 ft. wide, and 10 ft. deep. When full of water, what is the pressure on each side?

On one side, $12 \times 10 \times 5 \times 1{,}000$ oz. $= 600{,}000$ oz. $= 37{,}500$ lbs.
On one end, $6 \times 10 \times 5 \times 1{,}000$ oz. $= 300{,}000$ oz. $= 18{,}750$ lbs.

32. Why does a dead fish always float on its back?

It has its swimming-bladder located just under the spine; and this is the lightest part of its body, and, of course, comes to the top as soon as the fish dies.

34. A vessel holds 10 lbs. of water; how much mercury would it contain?

Mercury is 13.5 times heavier than water. Hence the vessel would contain 10 lbs. $\times 13.5 = 135$ lbs. of mercury.

35. A stone weighs 70 lbs. in air and 50 in water. What is its bulk?

$70 - 50 = 20$. 20×16 oz. $= 320$ oz., the weight of water displaced.
$$320 \text{ oz. is } \tfrac{8}{25} \text{ of a cu. ft.}$$

---

* In these solutions the student should notice that avoirdupois weight is used in weighing the gold. To be exact, 1,000 oz., the weight of a cu. ft. of water, should be reduced to Troy weight, and the lb. gold taken as 12 oz. Troy, when the answer would be about 1.36 cu. ft.

36. A hollow ball of iron weighs 10 lbs.: what must be its volume to float in water?

10 lbs. = 160 oz. As a cubic ft. of water weighs 1,000 oz., the ball must displace such a part of a cu. ft. of water as 160 oz. is of 1,000 oz., or .16 cu. ft.

37. Suppose that Hiero's crown was an alloy of silver and gold, and weighed 22 oz. in air and $20\frac{1}{4}$ oz. in water. What was the proportion of each metal?

"Multiply the specific gravity of each ingredient by the difference between it and the specific gravity of the compound. As the sum of the products is to the respective products, so is the specific gravity of the body to the proportions of the ingredients. Then, as the specific gravity of the compound is to the weight of the compound, so is each of the proportions to the weight of its material."—*American Cyclopedia.*

Second method:

Let A = mass of crown = 22
" B = sp. gr. " = 14.66
" x = mass of gold
" x' = sp. gr. " = 19.26
" y = mass of silver
" y' = sp. gr. " = 10.5

then
$$A = x + y;$$
and since
$$\text{volume} = \frac{\text{mass}}{\text{specific gravity}},$$
we have
$$\frac{A}{B} = \frac{x}{x'} + \frac{y}{y'};$$
whence we find (approximately),

Gold = 13.95
Silver = 8.05

121—38. Why will oil, which floats on water, sink in alcohol?

The specific gravity of absolute alcohol is only .79; hence even the dilute alcohol of commerce is lighter than most specimens of oil.

39. *A specific-gravity bottle holds 100 gms. of water and 180 gms. of sulphuric acid. Required the density of the acid.*—Ans. **1.8.**

40. *What is the density of a body which weighs 58 gms. in air and 46 gms. in water?*—Ans. **4⅚.**

41. *What is the density of a body which weighs 63 gms. in air and 35 gms. in a liquid of a density of .85?*—Ans. **1.9125.**

HYDRODYNAMICS.

129—1. *Two faucets, one 8 feet and the other 4 feet below the surface of the water in a cistern, are kept open for a minute. How many times as much water can be drawn from the first as the second?*

$$\frac{v}{v'} = \frac{\sqrt{2gh}}{\sqrt{2gh'}} = \frac{\sqrt{h}}{\sqrt{h'}} = \sqrt{\tfrac{8}{4}} = \sqrt{2} = 1.4142.$$

Hence the first delivers rather more than 41% more than the second.

2. *How much water will be discharged per second from a short pipe having a diameter of 4 inches and a depth of 48 feet below the surface of the water?*

The cross section of the pipe is $16 \times .7854 = 12.57$ sq. inches, $= .087$ sq. feet.
$$v = \sqrt{2gh} = \sqrt{64 \times 48} = 55.4$$
$$55.4 \times .087 = 4.8 \text{ cu ft.}$$

3. *When we pour molasses from a jug, why is the stream so much larger near the nozzle than at some distance from it?*

Because, according to the law of falling bodies, the farther the molasses falls the faster it falls. The stream, therefore, becomes smaller as it moves more swiftly, until, at last, it breaks up into drops.

4. *Ought a faucet to extend into a barrel beyond the staves?*

No; this would cause more friction, and increase the resistance to outflow produced by cross currents.

5. *What would be the effect if both openings in one of the arms of Barker's Mill were on the same side?*

It would cease revolving. The pressure in each direction would then be equal, and the arms would balance.

PNEUMATICS.

145—1. *Why must we make two openings in a barrel of cider when we tap it?*

One to let out the cider, and one to admit the air.

2. *What is the weight of 10 cubic feet of air?*

100 cu. in. weigh 31 grs.; hence 10 cu. ft. will weigh 31 grs. × 172.8 = .7652 lbs. avoirdupois.

3. *What is the pressure of the air on one square rod of land?*

$272\frac{1}{4} \times 144 \times 15$ lbs. = 588,060 lbs.

4. *What is the pressure on a pair of Magdeburg hemispheres 4 in. in diameter, when the air is entirely exhausted?*

On each hemisphere the pressure is equal to the area of a great circle, multiplied by the pressure on each unit of area. Hence on each hemisphere the pressure is

$.7854 \times 4^2 \times 15$ lbs. = 188.5 lbs. nearly.

The sum of the two opposite pressures is thus not quite 277 lbs.

5. *How high a column of water can the air sustain when the barometric column stands at 28 in.?*

28 in. × $13\frac{1}{2}$ = $31\frac{1}{2}$ feet.

6. *If we should add a pressure of two atmospheres, what would be the volume of 100 cu. in. of common air?*

The pressure is trebled, and, according to Mariotte's law, the volume will be reduced in the same proportion; hence it will be 100 cu. in. ÷ 3 = $33\frac{1}{3}$ cu. in.

146—7. *If, while the water is running through the siphon, we quickly lift the long arm, what will be the effect on the water in the siphon? If we lift the entire siphon?*

The question assumes the siphon to be flexible. If the bottom of the long arm be below that of the short arm, the water flows through it toward the lower level. By lifting it the rate of flow diminishes until its level is the same as that of the short arm. On lifting it still higher, the water contained in the siphon flows back through the short arm, and the siphon is thus emptied. If, however, the whole siphon is lifted, it is emptied through the long arm.

8. *When the mercury stands at $29\frac{1}{4}$ in. in the barometer, how high above the surface of the water can we place the lower pump-valve?*

In theory, $29\frac{1}{4}$ in. $\times 13\frac{1}{2} = 398\frac{1}{4}$ in.; in practice, the distance is much less than this.

9. *Can we raise water to a higher level by means of a siphon?*

There is no power in a siphon; it is only a way of guiding the flow of water to a lower level.

10. *If the air in the chamber of a fire-engine be condensed to $\frac{1}{16}$ its former bulk, what will be the pressure due to the expansive force of the air on every square inch of the air-chamber?—Ans.* **240 lbs.**

11. *What causes the bubbles to rise to the surface when we put a lump of loaf-sugar in hot tea?*

The bubbles of air contained in the pores of the sugar rise because they are lighter than the water.

12. *When will a balloon stop rising? What weight can it lift?*

It will stop rising when the weight of the balloon and its contents is just equal to that of the same volume of rarefied air which it displaces. It can lift a weight equal to the difference between the weight of the hydrogen or coal gas with which it is filled and that of the air in which it is immersed, minus the weight of the balloon itself.

14. When smoke ascends in a straight line, is it a proof of the rarity or density of the air?

Of its density, because it shows that the smoke is much lighter than the air, and so rises immediately.

15. Explain the action of the common leather-sucker.

There is nearly a vacuum between the sucker and the slab, which is buoyed up by the pressure of the air beneath.

16. Did you ever see a bottle really empty?

No. No absolute vacuum has ever been produced in a bottle or any other vessel by human agency, so far as is known.

18. How does the variation in the pressure of the air affect those who ascend lofty mountains? Who descend in diving bells?

The outward pressure at a great elevation is partly removed, and the inner pressure remaining the same, the blood is often forced through the ears, nostrils, etc. When one descends into a deep mine the conditions are reversed : the outer pressure becomes in excess of the inner ; severe pain is felt in the ear-drum, and ringing noises in the head become almost intolerable. These, however, disappear after a time, when the equilibrium between the internal and external pressure is restored. It is said that Humboldt ascended where the mercurial column fell to 14 inches, and descended in a diving-bell where it rose to 45 inches—thus making a variation of 31 inches, or a difference of 31,000 lbs. pressure on the body.

19. Explain the theory of "sucking cider" through a straw.

By the action of the muscles of the chest the lungs are made to expand. A partial vacuum in them is thus produced, and the pressure of the air hence forces liquid through the straw up into the mouth. By closing the glottis at the right moment this is prevented from going through the windpipe, and it is at once swallowed.

20. Would it make any difference in the action of the siphon if the limbs were of unequal diameter?

The flow of water through the narrower part of the siphon would be faster than through the wider part.

21. *What would be the effect of making a small hole in the top of a diving-bell while in use?*

It would allow the compressed air to be pushed out by the pressure of the water below.

22. *The pressure of the atmosphere being 1.03 kg. per sq. cm., what is the amount on 10 sq. meters?*

103,000 kg.

ACOUSTICS.

184—1. *Why can not the rear of a long column of soldiers keep time to the music?*

Because it takes time for the sound-wave to pass down the column, and hence those in the rear do not hear the music as soon as those in front.

2. *Three minutes elapse between the flash and the report of a thunderbolt: how far distant is it?*

If the air is at the freezing point, the distance is
$$1{,}090 \text{ ft.} \times 60 \times 3 = 196{,}200 \text{ ft.}$$

3. *Five seconds expire between the flash and report of a gun: what is the distance?*
$$1{,}090 \text{ ft.} \times 5 = 5{,}450 \text{ ft.}$$

4. *Suppose a speaking-tube should connect two villages 10 miles apart. How long would it take a sound to pass that distance?*
$$52{,}800 \text{ ft.} \div 1{,}090 \text{ ft.} = 48.4 \text{ (sec.)}$$

This is of course a theoretical case. The initial energy manifested as sound would be transformed into other modes of energy, such as heat, before complete transmission through so great a distance in a speaking-tube, unless the sound be more intense than that of the human voice usually is.

5. *The report of a pistol-shot was returned to the ear from the face of a cliff in 4 seconds. How far was it?*

$$1{,}090 \text{ ft.} \times 2 = 2{,}180 \text{ ft.}$$

6. *What is the cause of the difference in the voice of man and woman?*

Probably the difference depends largely on the thickness and length of the vocal chords. The difference between a bass and a tenor, a contralto and a soprano, depends largely also on quality, just as the sound of the flute and violin on the same note is recognizably different.

7. *What is the number of vibrations per second necessary to produce the fifth tone of the scale of C_2?*

$$C_2 = 256 \text{ vibrations.}$$
$$256 \times \tfrac{3}{2} = 384.$$

8. *What is the length of each sound-wave in that tone when the temperature is zero F.?*

$1{,}090$ ft. $- 32$ ft. $= 1{,}058$ ft. $1{,}058 \div 384 = 2$ ft. 9 in. (the length of each wave).

9. *What is the number of vibrations in the fourth tone above C_2?*

$$C_2 = 128 \text{ vibrations.}$$
$$128 \times \tfrac{3}{2} = 192.$$

10. *If a meteor were to explode at a height of 60 miles, would it be possible for its sound to be heard at sea-level?*

No. At such a height the atmosphere would be more rare than in the best vacuum ever produced by human means. The explosion would produce a sound far too faint to be audible.

11. *A stone is let fall into a well, and in four seconds is heard to strike the bottom; how deep is the well?*

Disregarding the minute interval required for the transmission of the sound,

$$S = \tfrac{1}{2}gt^2 = 16 \times 4^2 = 256 \text{ feet.}$$

12. What time would be required for a sound to travel five miles in the still water of a lake?

$$t = \frac{s}{v} = \frac{5 \times 5,280}{4,700} = 5.6 \text{ seconds.}$$

13. Does sound travel faster at the foot or at the top of a mountain?

The density and elasticity of the air vary in the same proportion; hence if the temperature were the same on top of a mountain that it is at the foot, the velocity of sound would be the same, but as it is always colder, the velocity is less.

14. Why is an echo weaker than the original sound?

Because the intensity of the sound-wave is weakened at each reflection. In addition to this, the sound which is perceived as an echo has traveled over a much greater distance than that which comes directly from the sonorous body.

15. Why is it so fatiguing to talk through a speaking-trumpet?

Because it is unusual, and unusual effort is necessary to secure adaptation to unusual conditions.

16. Why will the report of a cannon fired in a valley be heard on the top of a neighboring mountain better than one fired on the top of a mountain will be heard in the valley?

A sound always has the intensity given it by the density of the atmosphere where it originated, and not of that where it is heard.

(See Tyndall's *Lectures on Sound*, p. 40.)

17. Why do our footsteps in unfurnished dwellings sound so startlingly distinct?

In furnished rooms, the chairs, carpets, pictures, etc., break up the echoes. Then, also, our footsteps are louder on an uncarpeted floor.

18. Why do the echoes of an empty church disappear when the audience assemble?

The audience break up the echoes which interfere with the original sound. Wires strung across a lofty room often serve the same purpose to a slight extent.

19. What is the object of the sounding-board of a piano?

By its vibrations and those of the body of air which it incloses, it re-enforces the sound of the wires.

20. During some experiments, Tyndall found that a certain sound would pass through twelve folds of a dry silk handkerchief, but would be stopped by a single fold of a wet one. Explain.

(See Tyndall's *Lectures on Light*, p. 325, for a series of experiments showing the action of moisture on the propagation of sound-waves.)

21. What is the cause of the musical murmur often heard near telegraph lines?

It is produced by the vibration of the wires. These are thrown into motion by the wind and other causes.

22. Why will a variation in the quantity of water in a goblet, when caused to sound, make a difference in the tone?

It changes the area of the vibrating portion of the glass.

23. At what rate (in meters) will sound move through air at sea-level, the temperature being 20° C.?

Sound moves at the rate of 1,090 feet at 0° C. The difference is nearly 2 feet for each degree C.

$$1{,}090 \text{ feet} + 40 \text{ feet} = 1{,}130 \text{ feet.}$$

OPTICS.

235—1. Why is a secondary bow fainter than the primary?

The primary is produced by one reflection and two refractions; the secondary, by two reflections and two refractions. The additional reflection weakens the ray

Why are the colors reversed?

We can understand this by looking at Fig. 164. In one bow we see that the rays enter the drops at the top, and are refracted at the *bottom* to the eye; in the other, that the rays enter at the bottom, and are refracted at the *top* to the eye.

2. Why can we not see around a house or through a bent tube?

The rays of light move in straight lines.

3. What color would a painter use if he wished to represent an opening into a dark cellar?

Black.

4. Is black a color?

No; it is the absence of light, and hence of color.

Is white?

No. It is the result of mixing a multitude of tints, each of which loses its individuality as color by union with the rest.

5. By holding an object nearer a light, will it increase or diminish the size of the shadow?

It will increase it, because more rays are intercepted.

7. Where should we look for a rainbow in the morning?

In the west.

8. Can two spectators see the same rainbow?

They can not, because no two persons can be at the right angle to get the same color from a drop.

9. Why, when the drops of water are falling through the air, does the bow appear stationary?

Because amid the multitude of drops there are always some in the right direction.

10. Why can a cat see in the night better than a human being?

Because the pupils of its eyes are larger, and so admit more light.

11. Why can not an owl see distinctly in daylight?

Its eyes are adapted to faint light. That of bright sunshine is therefore too dazzling.

12. Why are we blinded when we pass quickly from a dark into a brilliantly lighted room?

The pupils of our eyes admit too much light, but they soon contract to the proper dimensions, and we can then see distinctly. When we pass out from a lighted room into a dark room, the conditions are reversed.

13. If the light on a distant planet is only $\frac{1}{100}$ that which we receive, how does its distance from the sun compare with ours?

As the intensity of light is inversely as the square of the distance, the distance is $\sqrt{100} = 10$ times as great as ours.

14. If when I sit 6 feet from a candle I receive a certain amount of light, how much will I diminish it if I sit back 6 feet farther?

As my distance from the light is doubled, the brightness is inversely as 2^2, or only $\frac{1}{4}$ as great.

15. Why do drops of rain, in falling, appear like liquid threads?

The impression the drop makes on the retina remains until the drop reaches the ground.

16. Why does a towel turn darker when wet?

More of the light is transmitted, and less reflected. We see this illustrated in greasing a bit of paper. It becomes semi-transparent because more light passes through it, but looks darker itself because less light is reflected to the eye.

17. Does color exist in the object or in the mind of the observer?

The property of absorbing energy of special wave length, and reflecting that of another wave length which we perceive as color, is a physical property of the object. The perception of this, as of sound, or of temperature, is finally a mental act.

18. *Why is lather opaque, while air and a solution of soap are each transparent?*

By repeated reflections and refractions in passing through the mass of lather, no ray can pass through in a straight line. Transparency is hence destroyed.

19. *Why does it whiten molasses candy to pull it?*

The viscous mass, by repeated pulling, becomes fibrous. The fibers at the surface reflect light more regularly, and hence the candy appears more nearly white.

20. *Why does plastering become lighter in color as it dries?*

Because, as the water evaporates, the mortar transmits less light, and reflects more light to the eye.

21. *Why does the photographer use a lamp with a chimney of red glass in the " dark room "?*

Because this glass transmits only the longer waves of light, while chemical effect is produced chiefly by the shorter waves.

22. *Is the common division of colors into " cold " and " warm " verified in philosophy?*

Yes; red contains more heat than violet.

23. *Why is the image on the camera, Fig. 177, inverted?*

The rays cross each other at the focus of the double convex lens.

24. *Why is the second image seen in the mirror, Fig. 140, brighter than the first?*

The first is formed by reflection from the glass, and the second from the mercury. As the latter is a better reflector, the second image will be brighter. Each image after that will be weakened by the repeated reflection.

27. Which will be seen at the greater distance, a yellow or a gray body?

The yellow, since it is brighter.

28. When a star is near the horizon, does it seem higher or lower than its true place?

Higher. The light in passing into our atmosphere, is refracted downward, and the star appears in the direction from which the ray enters the observer's eye.

29. Why can we not see a rainbow at midday?

Because the sun is not in the right position. To produce the ordinary rainbow, it must be toward the eastern or western horizon.

30. What conclusion do we draw from the fact that moonlight shows the same dark lines as sunlight?

That its light has the same source as that of the sun, and is, indeed, reflected sunlight.

31. Why does the bottom of a boat seen under clear water appear flatter than it really is?

Because, by refraction, the bottom of the boat is apparently elevated above its true place.

32. Of what shape does a round body appear in water?

It appears to be flattened; and hence a round body looks like an oval one.

33. Why is rough glass translucent while smooth glass is transparent?

The minute irregularities scatter the rays of light, and do not allow them to pass freely to the eye of the observer.

34. Why can a carpenter looking along the edge of a board tell whether it is straight?

If the edge is straight, the light will be reflected uniformly to his eye from the whole length. Any uneven places will make dark and light spots.

35. Why can we not see out of the window after we have lighted the lamp in the evening?

The glass reflects the light of the lamp back to our eyes, and they adapt themselves to the increased amount.

36. Why does a ground-glass globe soften the light?

It scatters the rays.

37. Why can we not see through ground-glass or painted windows?

They transmit the light irregularly to the eye, and not uniformly, like a transparent body.

38. Why does the moon's surface appear flat?

Because it is so distant that the eye can not detect the difference between the distance of the center and the circumference.

39. Why can we see farther with a telescope than with the naked eye?

Because it furnishes us more light with which to see a distant object.

40. Why is not snow transparent, like ice?

Because it is discontinuous, and the rays of light are broken by multitudinous reflections and refractions.

41. Are there rays in the sunbeam which we can not see?

We can not see the heat or the chemical rays.

42. Why, when we press the finger on one eyeball, do we see objects double?

Because the rays from the same external object fall on parts of the two retinas that do not correspond in position.

43. Why does a distant light, in the night, seem like a star?

Because its image on the retina is so small that deception becomes easy.

44. Why does a bright light, in the night, seem so much nearer than it is?

We judge of the distance of an object by its magnitude, by its distinctness of outline, and by the size, etc., of intervening objects with which we compare it. In the night, the brightness of a light confuses us by its vividness, seeming to be near at hand. Moreover, we can not see the neighboring objects, whose distance we know or could estimate in the daylight. Our error is therefore one of judgment.

45. What color predominates in artificial lights?
Yellow.

46. Why are we not sensible of darkness when we wink?
Because the wink does not last so long as the impression of the light received just before the wink.

47. Under what condition do the eyes of a portrait seem to follow a spectator to all parts of a room?
This is noticed only in a full-face portrait. In that case the spectator, when he goes to either side, fails to see the side of the eyeballs, and hence the effect is that of looking directly into the eye. "A rifleman, portrayed as if taking aim directly in front of the picture, appears to every observer to be pointing at him specially."

48. Why do the two parallel tracks of a railroad appear to approach in the distance?
The visual angle subtended by the distance between two opposite points on the tracks becomes less as the distance of the observer increases.

49. Why does a fog apparently magnify objects?
It is not the refraction of the rays of light, as is commonly supposed, which makes an object seem larger when seen through a mist. It really appears to us in its proper size. The mist, however, dims the color and the outline, giving it the indistinctness belonging to a mile in distance, while it has the magnitude of half a mile. Dr. Wayland relates that, as he was

sailing through Newport harbor early one morning, in a dense fog, he observed on the apparently distant wharf some very tall men. While he was remarking upon their extraordinary size, he was astonished to see them jumping about like children, and otherwise behaving in a most unaccountable manner. Presently, as the sun dispersed the fog, he found that he was close to the wharf, and that the gigantic men were really a party of small boys amusing themselves with play.

The opposite mistake is made when the atmosphere is more transparent than that to which we are accustomed. Foreign travelers in Switzerland, who have started on foot to visit a glacier or a mountain-peak which seemed within easy distance, have often been surprised to find, after two or three hours of brisk walking, that the object of their desire seemed as far away as at first. So in looking across a sheet of water, where there are no intervening objects, distance is always underrated.

When we throw a stone at an object in the water we find that our eye has deceived us, and the stone falls far short of the mark. For the same reason, objects seen on the shore from the water seem much less than their natural size. The fact is, they appear of the magnitude which belongs to the distance, but we suppose the distance less than it is; and, associating this magnitude with diminished distance, they appear to us less than they really are.

In order to form these judgments correctly, one of these elements must be fixed. From this we learn to institute a comparison, and thus form an accurate opinion. If we know the magnitude of an object, the change in its color and outline will teach us its distance. If we know its distance, we can judge of its magnitude. Hence, painters, in order to give us a correct idea of an object which they represent, always place in its vicinity something with whose real magnitude we are familiar. Thus, to show the size of a pyramid, an Arab with his camel may be drawn at its foot. If the pyramid were represented by itself, its intended size might be mistaken; but every one knows the size of a camel, and from this he would judge of the magnitude of a pyramid.—*Wayland's Intellectual Philosophy*, p. 78, *et seq.*

50. *If you sit where you can not see another person's image, why can not that person see yours?*

The angle of incidence is equal to the angle of reflection under all circumstances. If a ray from the other person is not reflected at the right angle to reach your eye, then a ray from you is not reflected at the right angle to reach the other person's eye.

51. *Why can we see the multiple images in a mirror better if we look into it very obliquely?*

More light is then reflected to the eye. The ratio of the light reflected to the light refracted increases with the angle of incidence.

52. *Why is an image seen in water inverted?*
(Examine Fig. 139 in *Physics*.)

53. *Why is the sun's light fainter at sunset than at midday?*
(See *Physics*, p. 191, note.)

54. *Why can we not see the fence-posts when we are riding rapidly?*

Because the images of a succession of objects are formed on the retina at intervals less than that of the duration of a retinal impression. Hence, they all become confused, and nothing is seen distinctly.

55. *Ought a red flower to be placed in a bouquet by an orange one? A pink or blue with a violet one?*
(See *Physics*, p. 217.)

These are not complementary colors, and hence do not strengthen each other by contrast.

56. *Why are the clouds white while the clear sky is blue?*

Prof. Tyndall has shown that the larger particles of vapor scatter light of all colors, *i.e.*, white light; while the smallest particles, only the blue rays. In accordance with this fact, the clouds are white and the sky is blue. If the air were absolutely pure, free from all foreign matter, and highly rarefied, it is thought that the azure of the sky would not be seen, and the heavens would appear black: the illumination of objects would be strong and glaring on one side, and on the opposite side the shadows would be deep and unrelieved by the diffused light to which we are accustomed. The minute particles of vapor in the air serve to scatter the direct rays of the sun, and to turn them around corners and into places not in the direct line of the sunlight.

(See a full and interesting discussion in Tyndall's *Lecture on Light*, p. 152, *et seq.*)

57. Why does skim-milk look blue and new milk white?

The fatty globules of the new milk reflect all the colors of the spectrum to the eye; but when deprived of the cream the milk reflects the blue light in excess of the others.

58. Why is not the image of the sun in water at midday so bright as near sunset?

The angle of incidence being small, most of the light is transmitted, and but little is reflected. Near sunset the greater part is reflected.

59. Why is the rainbow always opposite the sun?
(See *Physics*, p. 217.)

60. Hold a card with its edge close in front of your eye and look at a distant candle flame in a dark room. You will probably perceive either a reddish or a bluish fringe on one side. Explain.

The crystalline lens is not corrected for chromatic aberration. (See *Physics*, p. 219.)

HEAT.

273—1. *Why will one's hand, on a frosty morning, freeze to a metallic door-knob sooner than to one of porcelain?*

Because the metal is a better conductor of heat than the porcelain, and hence conducts the heat from the hand faster.

2. Why does a piece of bread toasting curl up on the side toward the fire?

The water being expelled from the pores on that side causes the bread to shrink.

3. Why do double windows protect from the cold?

The non-conducting air inclosed between the window-panes keeps in the heat and keeps out the cold.

4. Why do furnace-men wear flannel shirts in summer to keep cool, and in winter to keep warm?

In summer the non-conducting flannel keeps out the furnace-heat, and in the winter keeps in the body-heat.

5. Why do we blow our hands to make them warm, and our soup to make it cool?

Our breath is warmer than our hands, but cooler than our soup.

6. Why does snow protect the grass in winter?

The air inclosed between the flakes of snow is a non-conductor. No infant in its cradle is tucked in more tenderly than the coverlet of snow about the humble grass that nestles down for its winter's nap on the bosom of Mother Earth.

7. Why does water "boil away" more rapidly on some days than on others?

Because the atmospheric pressure varies, independently of the fact that the source of heat may vary without our noticing it.

8. What causes the crackling sound in a stove when a fire is lighted?

The expansion of the iron by the heat.

9. Why is the tone of a piano higher in a cold room than in a warm one?

The steel wires lengthen in a warm room, and so lower the tone.

10. Ought an inkstand to have a large or a small mouth?

A small mouth, to prevent evaporation.

11. Why is there a space left between the ends of the rails on a railroad track?

To allow room for the expansion and contraction of the rails with the changes in temperature.

12. Why is a person liable to take cold when his clothes are damp?

The water which evaporates from his clothes, in drying, absorbs heat from his body.

13. What is the theory of corn-popping?

The air in the cells of the corn expands by the heat, and bursts the outer coating of the corn.

14. Could vacuum-pans be employed in cooking?

They could not, because the heat would not be sufficient to cook the food.

15. Why does the air feel so chilly, in the spring, when snow and ice are melting?

When the ice is passing into the liquid state, it absorbs heat from all surrounding objects.

16. Why, in freezing ice-cream, do we put the ice in a wooden vessel, and the cream in a tin one?

The non-conducting wooden vessel prevents the ice from absorbing heat from the external air, and the conducting tin vessel enables it to absorb the heat from the cream.

17. Why does the temperature generally moderate when the snow falls?

The vapor passing into the solid form gives off heat.

19. Why does sprinkling a floor with water cool the air?

The water turning to vapor absorbs heat.

20. How low a degree of temperature can be reached with a mercurial thermometer?

Nearly to the freezing point of mercury,—39° F.

21. If the temperature be 70° F., what is it C.?

70° − 32° = 38°.   38 ÷ 1.8 = 21.1° C.

If the temperature be 70° C., what is it F.?

70° × 1.8 = 126°.   126° + 32° = 158° F.

22. Will dew form on an iron bridge?

Yes, because iron is a good radiator.

On a plank walk?

Not so readily, because wood is a poorer radiator.

23. Why will not corn pop when very dry?

The pores shrink, and the corn becomes compact; only porous, tender-celled corn will pop.

24. When the interior of the earth is so hot, why do we get the coldest water from a deep well?

The well extends below the influence of the sun, and not deep enough to be affected by the internal heat of the earth.

25. Ought the bottom of a tea-kettle to be polished?

No, since a polished surface would reflect the heat. We need a black, rough, sooty surface to absorb the heat rapidly.

26. Which boils the sooner, milk or water?

Milk, because it is so adhesive that the bubbles of steam which are formed at the bottom of the dish can not easily escape. They therefore pile up on top of each other, and the milk boils over readily.

27. Is it economy to keep our stoves highly polished?

The stove-blacking used is a good radiator, but the surface should not be highly polished, as that hinders radiation.

28. If a thermometer be held in a running stream, will it indicate the same temperature that it would in a pailful of the same water?

It will. For the same reason that a thermometer, in the wind, will indicate the same temperature as in the still air, although the former seems to us much colder.

29. Which makes the better holder when one wishes to protect his hands from a hot dish, woolen or cotton?

Woolen, because it is so poor a conductor of heat.

30. Which will give out the more heat, a plain stove or one with ornamental designs?

The latter, since it has more radiating surface.

31. Does dew fall?

No; it forms directly where it is found. The vapor merely collects on the cold surface.

32. What causes the "sweating" of a pitcher?

The vapor of the air condenses on the cold pitcher. It is often a sign of rain, since it shows that the air is full of vapor easily deposited.

33. Why is evaporation hastened in a vacuum?

Because the pressure of the air is removed.

34. Does stirring the ground around plants aid in the deposition of dew?

It does, since it facilitates radiation.

35. Why does the snow at the foot of a tree melt sooner than that in the open field?

The tree absorbs the sun's heat, and then radiates it out, thus serving as a carrier for the snow.

36. Why is the opening in a chimney made to decrease in size from bottom to top?

Because as the heated air rises it cools and shrinks. If the chimney did not diminish in size correspondingly, currents of cold air would set down from the top.

37. Will tea keep hot longer in a bright or in a dull tea-pot?

In a bright one, since a polished surface retards radiation.

38. What causes the snapping of wood when laid on the fire?
The expansion of the air in the cells of the wood.

39. Why is one's breath visible on a cold day?
The vapor in the breath is condensed by the cold air.

40. What gives the blue color to air?
The particles floating in it reflect the blue light of the sunbeam.

41. How does the heat at two feet from the fire compare with that at four feet?
$$2^2 : 4^2 :: 1 : 4.$$
Hence it is four times greater.

42. Why does the frost remain later in the morning upon some objects than upon others?
The best radiators are the best absorbers. They become warmed by the morning sun more quickly than the poorer radiators, and the frost on them is hence more quickly melted.

43. Is it economy to use green wood?
No. Its sap has to be changed to vapor, thus absorbing a large amount of energy at the expense of the combustion.

44. Why does not green wood snap?
The pores are filled with water instead of air. The water does not expand rapidly enough to burst off the coverings of the cells, and so simply oozes out gradually, and is vaporized.

45. Why will a piece of metal dropped into a glass or porcelain dish of boiling water facilitate the ebullition?
The rougher surface of the metal aids in the formation and disentanglement of the steam-bubbles. The bubbles cling longer to a smooth than to a rough surface. This is one cause of that bumping sound often noticed when liquids are boiling in glass dishes.

46. Which can be ignited the more easily with a burning-glass, black or white paper?

Black paper, since it is a much better absorber of heat.

47. Why does the air feel colder on a windy day?

Because fresh portions of cold air are brought constantly in contact with our bodies.

48. Could a burning-lens be made of ice?

Burning-lenses have been made of that material. The rays have no heating power until the waves of ether are stopped. They do not elevate the temperature of the medium through which they pass.

49. Why is an iceberg frequently enveloped by a fog?

The moisture of the air is condensed upon its cold surface.

50. Would dew gather more freely on a rusty stove than on a bright kettle?

It would, because the rusty iron surface is a good radiator.

51. Why is a clear night colder than a cloudy one during the same season?

On a cloudy night the clouds reflect the radiated heat of the earth back again, and thus act as a blanket to keep the earth warm. On such a night there can be no frost or dew. On a clear night, the heat which the earth radiates passes out freely into space, and thus the earth cools rapidly.

52. Why is no dew formed on cloudy nights?

See last question.

53. Why will "fanning" cool the face?

It brings in contact with the face a current of fresh and generally cooler air.

54. How are safes made fire-proof?

By filling the space between the inner and the outer iron plates with a non-conducting material, as plaster, etc., the safe is rendered nearly fire-proof.

55. Why can you heat water quicker in a tin than a china cup?

Because the metal is a better conductor of heat than the china.

56. Why will a woolen blanket keep ice from melting?

The woolen is a non-conductor of heat.

57. Does dew form under trees?

The trees reflect back the heat radiated by the earth, grass, etc., and so prevent the temperature, in general, from sinking to the dew-point.

58. What is the principle of heating by steam?

The steam is condensed in the pipes, and gives out as temperature the energy which had been previously absorbed in changing water to steam.

59. What is the cause of "cloud-capped" mountains?

The warm, moist air from the valleys rises against the mountain sides. Its vapor, previously invisible, becomes condensed by the colder air into a cloud of droplets that float in the air.

60. Show how the glass in a hot-house acts as a trap to catch the sunbeam.
(See *Physics*, p. 259.)

61. Does the heat of the sun come in through our windows?
(See *Physics*, p. 259.)

62. Does the heat of our stoves pass out in the same way?
(See *Physics*, p. 259.)

63. The top of a mountain is nearer the sun; why is it not warmer?
(See *Physics*, pp. 250 and 260.)

67. Can we find frost on the windows and on the stone-flagging the same morning?

It requires a much intenser cold to produce the former effect than the latter, as glass is a poorer conductor of heat than stone. We frequently find frost on the flagging early in the fall, but frost on the window is a sign of very severe winter weather.

68. Why will not snow "pack" into balls except in mild weather?

The snow must be very near the melting-point for the pressure of the hand to be sufficient to melt enough of it to produce the phenomena of regelation. (*Physics*, p. 271, 1st note; also Tait's *Recent Advances in Physical Science*, p. 129, and Tyndall's *Forms of Water*, p. 163.) This principle involves the theory of Glaciers. "The masses of snow can not rest on the steep slopes of Alpine summits. The pressure upon the under layers is too great to allow them to remain upon their sloping beds, and they are forced to descend. This descent is accomplished in two forms: that of an avalanche, one of the most awful and imposing spectacles to witness; or of a glacier, which is really an avalanche of ice of extremely slow motion. But the glacier differs from the ordinary avalanche not only in that its motion is so slow, but in that it consists of ice, thick, firm, and hard. The principles involved in this transition of the loose, flaky snow which first falls upon the mountain-top into the solid ice of the glacier, are very well illustrated, as Helmholtz has remarked, in the manufacture of the schoolboy's snow-ball or snow-man. Very cold snow is always light and flaky, and can not be made by the pressure of the hands into a cohesive mass; in order to succeed in that operation, snow is always employed which is already at the melting-point, or only so far below this temperature that the warmth of the hand suffices to bring it to the required temperature, and then, by dint of pressure and molding, an icy ball may be easily produced. So with the formation of the glacier ice. A process of almost simultaneous melting and freezing goes on among the under layers of snow, and under an immense and ever-constant pressure from the weight of the snow above; thus solid ice is formed. That this ice conforms itself to the various windings, constrictions, and dilatations of its rocky channel during its downward march, is a fact not less familiar than wonderful."

69. Why is the sheet of zinc under a stove so apt to become puckered?

When zinc cools after expansion it does not return quite to its former dimensions, and so becomes "puckered," as it is called.

70. Why does a mist gather in the receiver of the air-pump as the air becomes rarefied?

"The remaining air, cooled by rarefaction, absorbs heat from the invisible vapor in combination with it, and renders the water visible. The mist may be removed by continued action of the machine, or by re-admitting the normal quantity of air."

(See Arnott's *Physics*, p. 448.)

71. Why are the tops of high mountains in the tropics covered with perpetual snow?

See question 59.

MISCELLANEOUS QUESTIONS AND PROBLEMS FOR REVIEW.

1. Does a plumb-line point to the earth's center of figure or center of gravity?

2. In a dark room, let the light of a candle pass through a small hole in a card, and the image of the candle on the opposite wall will be inverted. Explain.

3. How many times heavier is the earth than an equally large globe of water?

4. Why does a rocket ascend into the air?

5. Is the water at the foot of Niagara Falls warmer than that in the river above?

6. What causes wheel fire-works to rotate?

7. A brass rod covered tightly with thin paper may be held some time in a flame without the paper being scorched; while, if the rod be of wood, the paper will scorch at once. Why is this difference?

MISCELLANEOUS QUESTIONS.

8. How would it affect the action of a siphon if it were carried up a mountain?

9. If a vessel of water containing a floating body be placed under the receiver of an air-pump, and the air gradually exhausted, what will be the effect on the floating body?

10. How will it change the height of the column of mercury in a barometer to incline the tube?

11. In the image of a written page seen in a mirror, why does the writing seem to slope?

12. Why does a coin placed in a tumbler look larger when the glass is full of water than when it is empty?

13. Two bodies of different volume weigh the same in water; which will weigh the more in mercury, the larger or the smaller?

14. How does the wind drift sand, snow, etc.?

15. Why does oil "still troubled waters"?

16. Why does crouching down at the highest points in a swing, and standing up at the lowest point, increase the velocity?

17. What difference would it make in the guinea-and-feather experiment to force into the tube additional air, instead of exhausting it, as ordinarily done?

ANSWERS

TO THE

PRACTICAL QUESTIONS AND PROBLEMS

IN

STEELE'S POPULAR CHEMISTRY.

[The large figures refer to the page of the *Chemistry*, and the small ones to the number of the questions.]

26—1. *What becomes of the water that "dries up"? Of the wood that "burns up"? Is there any destruction of the matter they contain?*

The water is changed into invisible vapor, and wafted thus away.

The wood is oxidized into CO_2 and H_2O, which mingle with the air. The ashes consist of SiO_2, K_2CO_3, and the oxides of any other elements present whose compounds with O are not gaseous.

There is no destruction of the matter contained.

2. *Where is the higher oxide formed, at the forge or in the pantry?*

There is more complete oxidation at the forge. At low temperatures, decomposition results often in complex products.

3. *Why is the blood red in the arteries, and dark in the veins?*

When specimens of venous and of arterial blood are subjected to chemical examination, the differences presented by their solid and fluid constituents are found to be very small and inconstant. As a rule, there is rather more water in arterial blood, and rather more fatty matter. But the gaseous contents of the two kinds of blood differ widely in the proportion which the carbonic acid gas bears to the oxygen; there being a smaller quantity of oxygen and a greater quantity of carbonic acid, in venous than in arterial blood. And it may be experimentally demonstrated that this difference in their gaseous contents is the only essential difference between venous and arterial blood. For if arterial blood be shaken up with carbonic acid, so as to be thoroughly saturated with that gas, it loses oxygen, gains carbonic acid, and acquires the hue and properties of venous blood; while, if venous blood be similarly treated with oxygen, it gains oxygen, loses carbonic acid, and takes on the color and properties of arterial blood.—HUXLEY'S *Lessons in Physiology.*

4. Do we need more O in winter than in summer?

Yes, if we are much exposed to the open air, and forced to take abundant exercise in order to keep warm.

5. Which would starve sooner, a fat man or a lean one?

The lean one. A superabundance of flesh, in a time of scarcity, is taken up by the absorbents and thrown into the circulation, thus supplying the place of food in nourishing the body.

6. How do teamsters warm themselves by slapping their hands together?

This exercise promotes the circulation of the blood, and its oxidation is thus quickened.

7. Could a person commit suicide by holding his breath?

Respiration is entirely independent of consciousness, as is seen in sleep, coma, etc. It may be interrupted for a few minutes, but no effort of the will can enable one to hold his breath until life is extinct. The desire for O, the *besoin de respirer*, or the respiratory sense, as it is called, becomes at last so great that the strongest resolution yields the struggle.

8. Why do we die when our breath is stopped?

"In asphyxia it is difficult to say which destroys life, the absence of oxygen or the presence of carbonic acid."—FLINT.

There is an absence of oxygen, so essential to every vital operation, and also an accumulation of carbonic acid in the system.

9. Why do we breathe so slowly when we sleep?

The circulation is less rapid, and various functions of the body are less active. There is hence less need for rapid oxidation.

10. How does a cold-blooded animal differ from a warm-blooded one?

In the imperfection with which the blood is oxygenated. The lungs are often of small capacity, and loose texture, and are sometimes wanting entirely. In reptiles a portion of the blood is not sent to the heart, and hence in the vessels there is a mixture of arterial and venous blood. The breathing is therefore slow, the motions are languid, and there is little heat.

11. Why does not the body burn out like a candle?

Because it is renewed by the processes of assimilation and nutrition as rapidly as it is destroyed by the waste of oxidation. Whenever the former are in excess we gain flesh; when the latter, we grow poor.

12. Do all parts of the body change alike?

The rate of change varies with the amount of oxidation, and that depends on the use of the organ. The right arm of the blacksmith must be transformed much more rapidly than the left.

13. What objects would escape combustion if the air were undiluted O?

Burnt bodies, *i.e.*, those which are already combined with oxygen.

14. Why is it difficult to obtain O from the air?

Because, although free from combination, it is intimately mixed with N.

15. What weight of O can be obtained from 10 grams of HgO?

$$HgO : O :: 10 : x.$$
$$216 : 16 :: 10 : x.$$
$$x = \frac{16 \times 10}{216} = .74+, \text{ grams.}$$

16. How much O can be obtained from 6 grams of $KClO_3$?

$$KClO_3 : O_3 :: 6 : x.$$
$$122.5 : 48 :: 6 : x.$$
$$x = \frac{48 \times 6}{122.5} = 2.35+, \text{ grams.}$$

17. How much $KClO_3$ would be needed to produce 2 kilograms of O?

$$O_3 : KClO_3 :: 2 : x.$$
$$48 : 122.5 :: 2 : x.$$
$$x = \frac{122.5 \times 2}{48} = 5.1+, \text{ kilograms.}$$

18. How much KCl would be formed in preparing 1 kilogram of O?

$$KClO_3 = KCl + O_3.$$

Hence,
$$O_3 : KCl :: 1 : x.$$
$$48 : 74.5 :: 1 : x.$$
$$x = \frac{74.5}{48} = 1.55+, \text{ kilograms.}$$

19. Is it probable that all the elements are discovered?

No. But all new elements lately discovered have proved to be chemical rarities. Probably all of the abundant and generally useful elements have been discovered.

20. Is heat produced by oxidation?

It is a *manifestation* of chemical change. In this sense it may be considered to be caused by it.

21. What is the difference between kinetic and potential energy?

Kinetic energy is energy of motion; potential energy is that of position. (Consult Steele's *Popular Physics.* p. 35.)

22. Why does running cause panting?

One of several causes is the need of more O to supply the increased oxidation in the blood necessitated by unusual exertion.

23. How does O give us strength?

Our muscles, as well as the food from which they are formed, consist of complex molecules. When they are oxidized, potential energy becomes kinetic.

24. Does the plant produce energy?

No; it only absorbs solar energy, and becomes the medium of its transformation.

25. If we burn an organic body in a stove it gives off heat; in the animal body it produces also motion. Explain.

The force set free by the oxidation of the muscles, and of the food within the body, is converted into muscular energy.

26. Why does not blowing cold air on a fire with a bellows extinguish it?

It may extinguish it if the blast be strong enough. If not strong enough to cool it below its kindling point, the heat of oxidation more than balances the cooling from the air.

27. Why does blowing on a fire kindle it, and on a lighted lamp extinguish it?

The answer to the previous question applies to this one also.

28. Why can we not ignite hard coal with a match?

The heat of the match is not enough to decompose the coal, and thus set free gaseous constituents for the production of flame.

29. Why will an excess of coal put out a fire?

The coal is heated at the expense of the fire, and may reduce this below the kindling point unless the supply of O is rapid.

30. Could a light be extinguished by merely lowering the temperature?

Yes; by contact of a large body that is a good conductor of heat.

31. Why is it beneficial to stir a wood-fire, but not one of anthracite coal?

The gaseous constituents of wood are more easily separated than those of coal, but the heat evolved in combustion is less. When once well started, the combustion of the coal is hence more apt to be self-sustaining.

32. Why will water put out a fire?

It absorbs more heat in proportion to its weight than any other known substance does in changing from liquid to gas. The production of steam is hence at the expense of the heat of combustion, and the fuel is soon cooled below its kindling point.

33. What should we do if a person's clothes take fire?

Smother the flame by wrapping the person as quickly as possible with a rug, coat, blanket, or any thing of this kind that may be at hand. If water be near, throw it abundantly on the burning garment.

34. Ought the doors of a burning house to be thrown open?

No, except for the purpose of getting out of it. The increased supply of air through the opening promotes the combustion.

35. How much O can be obtained from 100 grams of HgO?

$HgO : O :: 100 : x.$
$216 : 16 :: 100 : x.$
$x = 7.4+$, grams.

36. What would be the volume of the O of Question 35 under the standard conditions?

$7.4 \div 1.43 = 5.17$ liters.

37. What would be the volume of the O at 12° C. and under a pressure of 740 mm. of mercury?

$$x = \frac{285}{273} \times \frac{760}{740} \times 5.17 = 5.42+, \text{ liters.}$$

38. *What would be the volume of the O of Question 16 at 20° C. and 750 mm.?*

$$x = \frac{1.55}{1.43} \times \frac{293}{273} \times \frac{760}{750} = 1.35+, \text{ liters.}$$

39. *How much $KClO_3$ must be employed to make an amount of O which shall measure 100 liters at 18° C. and 760 mm.?*

First find how many liters of O under standard conditions would be expanded to 100 liters at 18° C., the given pressure, 760 *mm.*, being itself standard. Call the result V. It is

$$V = \frac{273 \times 100}{291}.$$

Each of these liters weighs 1.43 grams; hence, the total weight is

$$W = \frac{27{,}300 \times 1.43}{291}.$$

Let $x =$ the required weight of $KClO_3$.

Then $\quad\quad\quad\quad O_2 : KClO_3 :: W : x.$

$$48 : 122.5 :: \frac{27{,}300 \times 1.43}{291} : x.$$

Hence,
$$x = \frac{27{,}300 \times 1.43 \times 122.5}{291 \times 48}.$$

$$x = 342.4 \text{ grams.}$$

37—1. *How could you detect any free O in a jar of N?*

By passing into it some NO (see p. 34). It will combine with the free O, forming red fumes of NO_2.

2. *How would you remove the product of the test?*

By allowing the mixture to stand over water, which will dissolve the NO_2.

3. *In the experiment shown in Fig. 9, why is the gas red in the flask, but colorless when it bubbles up into the jar?*

In the flask, one fifth of the atmosphere was free O, which produces NO_2 with the NO as soon as this is evolved. In the jar there is no free O.

4. How much NH_3 can be obtained from 3 grams of sal-ammoniac?

From the reaction, $2NH_4Cl + CaO = 2NH_3 + H_2O + CaCl_2$, we see that for every molecule of NH_4Cl used we obtain one molecule of NH_3. Hence,

$$NH_4Cl : NH_3 :: 3 : x.$$
$$53.5 : 17 \quad :: 3 : x.$$
$$x = .95+, \text{ gram.}$$

5. What will be the volume of the NH_3 at 20° C. and 770 mm.?

Taking H as our standard, the density of NH_3 is half its molecular weight, or $\dfrac{14+3}{2}, = 8.5$. The density of O is 16, and a liter of it weighs 1.43 grams. Hence, a liter of NH_3 weighs $\dfrac{8.5}{16} \times 1.43$ grams, or almost exactly .76 gram. The volume occupied by .95 gram of NH_3 under standard conditions is hence $\dfrac{.95}{.76}$ of a liter, or 1.25 liters. At 20° C. and 770 mm. the required volume will be

$$x = \frac{293}{273} \times \frac{760}{770} \times 1.25.$$
$$x = 1.324 \text{ liters.}$$

6. How much H_2O will be formed in the process?

From the reaction we see that one molecule of H_2O is formed for two molecules of NH_4Cl. Hence,

$$2NH_4Cl : H_2O :: 3 : x.$$
$$107 : 18 \quad :: 3 : x.$$
$$x = .5+, \text{ gram.}$$

7. How much CaO will be needed?

From the reaction we see that one molecule of CaO is required with two molecules of NH_4Cl. Hence,

$$2NH_4Cl : CaO :: 3 : x.$$
$$107 : 56 :: 3 : x.$$
$$x = 1.57 \text{ grams.}$$

8. How much N_2O can be made from 1 gram of ammonium nitrate?

The reaction is
$$NH_4NO_3 = 2H_2O + N_2O.$$
Hence,
$$NH_4NO_3 : N_2O :: 1 : x.$$
$$80 : 44 :: 1 : x.$$
$$x = .55 \text{ gram.}$$

9. How much nitric acid can be formed from 50 kilos of sodium nitrate ($NaNO_3$)?

The reaction is
$$2NaNO_3 + H_2SO_4 = Na_2SO_4 + 2HNO_3.$$
Hence,
$$NaNO_3 : HNO_3 :: 50 : x.$$
$$85 : 63 :: 50 : x.$$
$$x = 37+, \text{ kilograms.}$$

10. What causes flesh to decompose so much more easily than wood?

It is partly owing to the greater complexity of its molecule, and partly to the presence of the N, which is very unstable in its compounds.

11. If a tuft of hair be heated in a test tube, the liquid formed will turn red litmus-paper blue. Explain.

Ammonia is formed by the decomposition of the hair, and this acting on the red litmus-paper, turns it blue.

12. Why should care be used in opening a bottle of strong H_3N in a warm room?

The space above the liquid is filled with ammonia gas, which had been dissolved in the water at a low temperature. Its expansive force is greatly increased when the temperature is raised. When the stopper is removed, therefore, a concussion may result.

13. What weight of N is there in 10 grams of HNO_3?

$HNO_3 : N :: 10 : x.$
$63 : 14 :: 10 : x.$
$x = 2.2$ grams.

14. How much sal-ammoniac would be required to make 20 liters of NH_3 measured at 25° C. and 744 mm.?

Refer to the answer of Question 5. A liter of NH_3 under standard conditions weighs .76 gram.

First find how many liters of NH_3 at 0° C. and 760 *mm.* are required to expand to 20 liters at 25° C. and 744 *mm.* Call the result V. Then

$$V = \frac{273}{298} \times \frac{744}{760} \times 20 \text{ liters.}$$

Each of these weighs .76 gram. Call the result W.
Then $NH_3 \cdot NH_4Cl :: W : x.$

$$17 : 107 :: \frac{273 \times 744 \times 20 \times .76}{298 \times 760} : x.$$

$$x = \frac{107 \times 273 \times 744 \times 20 \times .76}{17 \times 298 \times 760}.$$

$x = 85.8$ grams.

15. What is the difference between liquid ammonia and liquor ammoniæ?

Liquid ammonia is the result of condensing the gas by cold. Liquor ammoniæ is the commercial name often applied to the solution of the gas in water.

52—1. Why, in filling the hydrogen gun, do we use 5 parts of common air to 2 of H, and only one part of O to 2 of H?

Because the air is only $\frac{1}{5}$ oxygen, and hence 5 parts of common air are equivalent to 1 part oxygen.

2. Why are coal cinders often moistened with H_2O before using?

(See *Popular Chemistry*, p. 45, note.)

The H_2O being decomposed by the heat of the fire increases the combustion.

3. What injury may be done by throwing a small quantity of H_2O on a fire?

"No more heat is produced by the action of the H_2O, but it is in a more available form for communicating heat. The steam in contact with incandescent charcoal is decomposed—the O going to the C to form CO_2, and the H being set free. If the C is abundant, and the heat high, the CO_2 is also decomposed, and double its volume of CO formed. The inflammable gases, H and CO, mingled with the hydrocarbons always produced, are ignited, making the billows of flame which sweep over a burning building."—S. P. SHARPLES.

4. Why does the hardness of water vary in different localities?

The hardness of the water will necessarily vary with the *solubility* of the minerals in different localities.

5. What causes the variety of minerals in the ocean? Is the quantity increasing?

The ocean contains the washings of the land. Every mineral soluble in water is borne to the sea. The quantity of mineral matter in the ocean would therefore seem to be increasing, yet there is a compensation in the return to the soil, of guano, marine plants, and fish, which are driven on shore by winds and waves, or carried by the industry of man.

Analysis of sea-water (Schweitzer):

Water	963.74
Sodium chloride	28.05
Potassium chloride	.76
Magnesium chloride	3.66
Magnesium bromide	.02
Magnesium sulphate	2.29
Calcium sulphate	1.40
Calcium carbonate	.03
Iodine	traces
Ammonia	traces
	1,000.00

6. Is there not a compensation in the sea-plants, fish, etc., which are washed back on the land?

(See Answer to Question 5.)

7. Since "all the rivers flow to the sea," why is it not full?

Because of the constant evaporation from its surface.

8. What is the cause of the tonic influence of the sea-breeze?

There are traces of certain minerals which probably give to the sea-breeze a bracing influence. The air from the ocean is also, doubtless, highly ozonized. It is free from the contaminations that so often make the atmosphere of the cities and parts of the country unhealthy.

9. When fish are taken out of the water, and thus brought into a more abundant atmosphere, why do they die?

Fish inhale O through the fine, silky filaments of their gills. When a fish is drawn out of H_2O, these dry up, and it is unable to breathe, although it is in a more plentiful atmosphere than it is accustomed to enjoy.

10. Do all fish die when brought on land?

No. Some fish have an apparatus for moistening their gills. They can therefore crawl about in the grass, and even migrate from one stream to another.

11. What weight of water is there in 100 lbs. of sodium sulphate (Na_2SO_4, $10H_2O$), or Glauber's salt?

$$10H_2O : Na_2SO_4, 10H_2O :: x : 100 \text{ lbs.}$$
$$180 : \quad 322 \quad :: x : 100 \text{ lbs.}$$
$$322\ x = 18,000 \text{ lbs.}$$
$$x = 55.9 \text{ lbs. } (H_2O).$$

12. What weight of water in a ton of alum (KAl, $2SO_4$, $12H_2O$)?

$$12H_2O : KAl, 2SO_4, 12H_2O :: x : 2,000 \text{ lbs.}$$
$$216 : \quad 474.5 \quad :: x : 2,000 \text{ lbs.}$$
$$474.5\ x = 432,000 \text{ lbs.}$$
$$x = 910.4 \text{ lbs. } (H_2O).$$

13. How does the air purify running water?

The O contained in the air absorbed by the H_2O oxidizes the organic substances, which are the most dangerous impurities.

14. *What is the action of potassium permanganate as a disinfectant?*

It gives up its O to oxidize the organic impurities.

15. *What weight of H can be obtained from a liter of water?*

The weight of a liter of water under standard conditions is 1,000 grams. Of this $\frac{1}{9}$ is H. Hence, the required weight is $111\frac{1}{9}$ grams.

16. *How much Zn must be employed to obtain 100 grams of H from H_2SO_4?*

The reaction is
$$Zn + H_2SO_4 = ZnSO_4 + 2H.$$
Hence,
$$2H : Zn :: 100 : x.$$
$$2 : 65 :: 100 : x.$$
$$x = 3{,}250 \text{ grams.}$$

17. *A liter of H under standard conditions weighs 0.0896 gram. What volume of H at 10° C. and 738 mm. can be obtained from H_2SO_4, by the action of 8 kilos of Zn?*

$$Zn + H_2SO_4 = ZnSO_4 + 2H.$$
$$Zn : 2H :: 8{,}000 : x \text{ in grams.}$$
$$65 : 2 :: 8{,}000 : x.$$
$$x = 246.15 \text{ grams.}$$

The number of liters under standard conditions is
$$\frac{246.15}{.0896}.$$

At 10° C. and 738 *mm.*, the volume is
$$V = \frac{246.15}{.0896} \times \frac{283}{273} \times \frac{760}{738}.$$
$$V = 2932.7 \text{ liters.}$$

18. *How much $KClO_3$ would be required to evolve sufficient O to burn the H produced by the decomposition of 2 grams of H_2O?*

The weight of H from 2 grams of H_2O is $\frac{2}{9}$ gram. The weight of O required to unite with it is $8 \times \frac{2}{9}$, or $\frac{16}{9}$ gram.

$$KClO_3 = KCl + 3O.$$
$$3O : KClO_3 :: \tfrac{16}{9} : x.$$
$$48 : 122.5 :: \tfrac{16}{9} : x.$$
$$x = 4.537 \text{ grams}.$$

19. How much O would be required to oxidize the metallic Cu which could be reduced from its oxide by passing over it, when white-hot, 20 grams of H gas?

The amount required to oxidize the Cu is obviously the same as that which would be separated from the CuO by reduction. The number of grams of O thus separated must be 8 times the weight of the H, or 160 grams.

20. How much O would be required to oxidize the metallic Fe which could be reduced in the same manner by 10 grams of H gas?

To oxidize 10 grams of H would require 80 grams of O. If this be withdrawn from the oxide of iron, the same amount would be required to oxidize the iron thus reduced.

21. Why are rose-balloons so buoyant?

Because the H which they contain displaces air that is more than 14 times as heavy.

22. How much H must be burned to produce a ton of water?

A ton is 2,000 pounds. The weight of H in a ton of water is $\frac{1}{9} \times 2{,}000$, or $222\frac{2}{9}$ pounds. To find the volume of this we remember that the weight of 100 cubic inches of air is 31 grains (see *Popular Physics*, p. 131). In every 5 parts of air there are 4 parts of N, weighing 14 times as much as the same volume of H, and 1 part of O, weighing 16 times as much; $\frac{(4 \times 14) + 16}{5}$ = 14.4, nearly. Hence, air is about 14.4 times as heavy as H. Therefore 31 grains will be the weight of 100×14.4 cubic inches of H, or of $\frac{1{,}440}{1{,}728}$ of a cubic foot of H. To reduce the given weight, $222\tfrac{2}{3}$ pounds, to grains, we multiply by 7,000, the number of grains in a pound, making $\dfrac{14,000,000}{9}$ grains.

Then $31 : \dfrac{14,000,000}{9} :: \dfrac{1,440}{1,728} : x$ in cubic feet.

$$x = 41,817 \text{ cubic feet.}$$

This would be enough to fill a spherical balloon 43 feet in diameter.

84—1. Why will pine-wood ignite more easily than maple?

It is richer in hydrocarbons, that are readily volatile.

2. Why is fire-damp more dangerous than choke-damp?

Fire-damp, CH_4, contains no O. At the appropriate temperature of kindling, when mixed with air, it is a dangerous explosive. Choke-damp, CO_2, is already a stable compound containing the largest proportion of O that can unite with C. It is, therefore, not explosive.

3. Represent the reaction in making CO_2, showing the atomic weights, as in the preparation of O on page 12.

$$CaCO_3 + 2HCl = CaCl_2 + H_2O + CO_2.$$
$$(40+12+48)+2(1+35.5) = (40+71)+(2+16)+(12+32).$$
$$100+73 = 111+18+44.$$
$$173 = 173.$$

4. Should one take a light into a room where the gas is escaping?

No. An important constituent of illuminating gas is the dreaded fire-damp, CH_4. Mixed with the air in the room, it may be exploded by introducing a lighted match or candle.

5. Why does it dull a knife to sharpen a pencil?

The particles of graphite in the pencil are very hard, and the knife edge is worn away by friction.

6. Where was the C, now contained in the coal, before the Carboniferous age?

Probably most of it was combined with O, forming CO_2 in a densely charged atmosphere.

7. *Must the air have then contained more plant food?*

Probably it did.

8. *What is the principle of the aquarium?*

The inter-dependence of animals and plants, whereby each supplies the wants of the other. The aquarium is a microcosm —a world in miniature.*

---

*I have read somewhere a beautiful Persian fable in which a nightingale and a rose are represented as being confined in a cage together, and being dependent upon each other for life. The fable is truth symbolized. The idea has now become more practical, but not less beautiful. In the modern aquarium, or drawing-room fish-pond, we see the world in miniature. It is a self-regulating, self-subsisting establishment, and is constructed on the most perfect principles of chemical economy.

"Before this truth of compensation between animals and plants was discovered, many attempts were made to keep fish in small glass globes. As they soon exhausted the oxygen, and impregnated the water with carbonic acid, it was necessary to change it daily. Finally, but a few years since, it was discovered that plants evolve oxygen and consume carbonic acid in the water as well as in the air. Starting out with this idea, about the year 1850, a Mr. Warrington, an Englishman, set about breeding fish and mollusks in tanks by the aid of marine plants. He succeeded admirably for a few days, but after a time a change came over his little world. Without apparent reason, the water became suddenly impure, and the fish died. Here was a new agency at work. With the aid of a microscope, Mr. Warrington explored his tank for the poison that was evidently latent there. He soon discovered that some of his plants had reached maturity, and, in obedience to the law of nature, had died. The decaying matter was the poison of which he was in search. How was this to be counteracted? In nature's tanks—seas, rivers, and ponds—reflected Mr. Warrington, plants must die and decay, yet this does not destroy animal life. We must see how nature remedies the evil. He hastened to a pond in the vicinity, and examined its bottom with care. He found, as he had anticipated, an abundance of vegetable matter decayed. He likewise found swarms of water-snails doing duty as scavengers, and devouring the putrefying substances before they had time to taint the water. Here was the secret; so beautiful a contrivance that it is said Mr. Warrington burst into tears when it flashed upon him like a revelation.

"He, however, quickly dried his eyes, gathered a quantity of snails, and threw a handful into his little tank at home. In a single day the water was clear and pure again. The fish throve and gamboled, grew and multiplied; the plants resumed their bright colors, and the snails not only rollicked in an abundance of decaying branches, but laid a profusion of eggs, on which the fish dined sumptuously every day."

9. What test should be employed before going down in an old well or cellar?

A lighted candle should be lowered. If that is dimmed or extinguished, it is not safe for one to descend.

10. What causes the sparkle of wine and the foam of beer?

The CO_2 formed in the process of fermentation.

11. What causes the cork to fly out of a catsup bottle?

The CO_2 which is produced when the catsup ferments.

12. What physical principle does the solidification of CO_2 illustrate?

That evaporation is a cooling process. A portion of the liquid CO_2 turns to vapor, and thus abstracts so much heat from the remainder as to freeze it. (See *Popular Physics*, p. 255.)

13. Why does the division in the chimney shown in Fig. 29 produce two currents?

For a few moments there is an uncertainty—a condition of unstable equilibrium. The heated air is tending to rise, and the cold air tending to come in to supply its place. The situation of the candle in the jar determines the length of time before the currents start. If the candle be placed on one side of the jar, they will be established almost instantly.

14. What causes the unpleasant odor of coal-gas? Is it useful?

Impurities which it contains. Olefiant gas has a faint sweetish odor, while carbonic oxide and hydrogen, when pure, are inodorous. The disagreeable smell is due in part to acetylene (C_2H_2). The unpleasant odor warns us of the presence of coal-gas.

15. What causes the sparkling often seen in a gas-light?

Particles of solid taken up mechanically in the process of purification, or otherwise.

16. Why does H in burning give out more heat than C?

1 lb. of H burned in O emits heat sufficient to melt 315.2 lbs. of ice; and 12 lbs. of carbon converted into CO_2 enough to melt 700 lbs. of ice. (This subject is quite fully treated in *Miller's Chemical Physics*, page 294, *et seq.*) The cause is not as yet fully determined, although it is perhaps safe to say that in ordinary combustion the heat depends on the amount of O which enters into combination with the fuel.

17. Why do not stones burn as well as wood?

Because they are already burned, *i.e.*, combined with O.

18. Why does not hemlock make good coals?

Because (1) of its lack of C, and (2) its porous structure.

19. What adaptation of chemical affinities is shown in a light?

If O had the same affinity for C that it has for H, they would be consumed at once, with little light. The fact that the H burns first, and thus heats up to the luminous point the particles of C as they float outward to the air, causes the illuminating power of the hydro-carbons.

20. Why does snuffing a candle brighten the flame?

Because it removes the charred wick, which diminishes the heat of the flame by both conduction and radiation.

21. Why is the flame of a candle red or yellow, and that of a kerosene oil-lamp white?

(See *Popular Physics*, p. 243).

The heat of a candle-flame is much less than that of kerosene, and thus the colors characteristic of a lower temperature are produced.

22. Why does a street gas-light burn blue on a windy night? Is the light then as intense? The heat?

O is mingled with the flame in sufficient quantities to burn the H and C simultaneously. Thereby the heat is increased, but the light diminished. The principle is that of Bunsen's burner.

23. *Why does not the lime burn in a calcium-light?*

Lime is a burned body; its symbol is CaO.

24. *Why is a candle-flame tapering?*
(See *Chemistry*, p. 77.)

The currents of air rushing toward the flame from all sides give it the conical form.

25. *Why does a draught of air cause a light to smoke?*

It lowers the heat of the flame below the point of union between C and O, and thus the C is precipitated.

26. *What makes the coal at the end of a candle-wick?*

The wick at the edge of the flame comes in contact with the O of the air, and therefore burns.

27. *Which is the hottest part of a flame?*

Toward the point of the cone, where the gaseous envelopes meet and make a solid flame.

28. *Why does not a candle-wick burn except at the edge of the flame?*

There is no O at the center of the flame.

29. *How does a chimney enable us to burn without smoke highly carboniferous substances like oil?*

It prevents the heated products of combustion from becoming mixed with cold air. These rise, and new air can come in only at the bottom. The stronger the heat in the chimney the greater is this draught. A flame, in which the combustion is imperfect when O is supplied slowly, becomes much brighter when O is supplied fast enough to produce perfect combustion of the H, and also to oxidize all the C without allowing any to pass off as smoke.

30. *How much CO_2 in 200 lbs. of chalk?*

$CO_2 : CaCO_3 :: x : 200$ lbs.
$44 : 100 :: x : 200$ lbs.
$100\ x = 8,800$ lbs.
$x = 88$ lbs. (CO_2).

31. What weight of CO_2 in a ton of marble?

$CO_2 : CaCO_3 :: x : 2,000$ lbs.
$44 : 100 :: x : 2,000$ lbs.
$100\ x = 88,000$ lbs.
$x = 880$ lbs. (CO_2).

32. Why does not a cold saucer held over an alcohol flame blacken, as it does over a candle or gas-light?

There is less C in alcohol than in tallow or in coal-gas.

33. How much CO_2 is formed in the combustion of one ton of C?

$C : CO_2 :: 2,000$ lbs. $: x$.
$12 : 44 :: 2,000$ lbs. $: x$.
$12\ x = 88,000$ lbs.
$x = 7333.33 +$ lbs. (CO_2).

34. What weight of C is there in a ton of CO_2?

$C : CO_2 :: x : 2,000$ lbs.
$12 : 44 :: x : 2,000$ lbs.
$44\ x = 24,000$ lbs.
$x = 545.45 +$ lbs. (C).

35. How much O is consumed in burning a ton of C?

In any quantity of CO_2, $\frac{8}{11}$ of the compound is O, and $\frac{3}{11}$ C. If $\frac{3}{11} = 2,000$ lbs. (CO_2), then $\frac{8}{11} = \frac{8}{3}$ of 2,000 lbs. $= 5333.33 +$ lbs. (O).

36. What weight of sodium carbonate (Na_2CO_3, 10 H_2O, " carbonate of soda ") would be required to evolve 12 grams of CO_2?

$CO_2 : Na_2CO_3\ 10H_2O :: 12$ gm. $: x$.
$44 : 286 :: 12$ gm. $: x$.
$44\ x = 2,432$ gm.
$x = 50.72$ gm. (Na_2CO_3, $10H_2O$).

37. How much CO_2 will be formed in the combustion of 30 gm. of CO?

$$CO : CO_2 :: 30 \text{ gm.} : x.$$
$$28 : 44 :: 30 \text{ gm.} : x.$$
$$28\,x = 1{,}320 \text{ gm.}$$
$$x = 47.14 \text{ gm. } (CO_2).$$

38. What weight of $CaCO_3$ would be required to evolve 12 grams of CO_2?

$$CaCO_3 + 2HCl = CaCl_2 + H_2O + CO_2.$$
$$CO_2 : CaCO_3 :: 12 : x.$$
$$44 : 100 :: 12 : x.$$
$$x = 27\tfrac{3}{11} \text{ grams.}$$

39. What would be the volume of these 12 grams of CO_2 at 12° C. and 744 mm.?

The molecular weight of CO_2 [12+2(16)], is 44. Its density is therefore 22. Under standard conditions 1 liter of H weighs .0896 gm.; therefore 1 liter of CO_2 weighs 22 × .0896 gm., or 1.97 gm. The number of liters that would weigh 12 gm. is hence $\frac{12}{1.97}$, or 6.09 liters. At 12° C. and 744 $mm.$ this volume would be expanded to

$$V = \frac{285}{273} \times \frac{760}{744} \times 6.09.$$
$$V = 6.494 \text{ liters.}$$

40. How much C would be necessary to furnish CO_2 enough to fill a gas-holder 10 meters high and 4 meters in diameter when the temperature is 25° C., and the barometer stands 754 mm.?

First find the capacity of the gas-holder. The volume of a cylinder is equal to its length multiplied by the area of its cross action. In this case it is $10 \times 3.1416 \times (2)^2$, or 125.664 cubic meters. Since in a cubic meter there are 1,000 liters, this volume is 125,664 liters, the temperature being 25° C., and the pressure 754 $mm.$ Reducing this to standard conditions, we have
$$V = 125{,}664 \times \frac{273}{298} \times \frac{754}{760}.$$
$$V = 114{,}210.5 \text{ liters.}$$

Each of these liters of CO_2 weighs 1.97 gm. (see answer to Question 39). Hence the total weight of CO_2 is 114,210.5 × 1.97 = 224,995 gm.

$$CO_2 : C :: 224,995 : x.$$
$$44 : 12 :: 224,995 : x.$$
$$x = 61.362\tfrac{8}{11} \text{ grams.}$$
Or $\qquad x = 61.362+, \text{ kilograms.}$

41. Write in double columns the different properties of carbon dioxide and carbon monoxide; thus,

CO_2 is 1, non-inflammable.	CO is 1, inflammable.
2. Atomic weight—44.	2. Atomic weight—28.
3. Specific gravity—1.529.	3. Specific gravity—.967.
4. Will not burn.	4. Burns with a blue flame.
5. A negative poison.	5. A direct poison.
6. Liquefies at 32°, and a pressure of 38.5 atmospheres.	6. Has never been liquefied.
7. Freely soluble in H_2O.	7. Sparingly soluble in water.
8. Forms salts.	Etc., etc.
Etc., etc.	

110—1. If chlorine water stands in the sunlight for a time, it will only redden a litmus-solution. Why does it not bleach it?

Hydrochloric acid is formed, which reddens the litmus.

2. Why do tinsmiths moisten with HCl, or sal-ammoniac, the surface of metals to be soldered?

It dissolves the coating of oxide, and leaves the surface of the metal free for the action of the solder.

3. How much HCl can be made from 25 kilos of common salt?
$$NaCl : Cl :: 25 : x.$$
$$58.5 : 35.5 :: 25 : x.$$
$$x = 15.17 \text{ kilograms.}$$

4. What weight of NaCl would be required to form 25 kilos of HCl?

$2NaCl + H_2SO_4 = Na_2SO_4 + 2HCl$.

Each molecule of NaCl thus yields one molecule of HCl.

$HCl : NaCl :: 25 : x$.
$36.5 : 58.5 :: 25 : x$.
$x = 40+$, kilograms.

5. *HCl of a specific gravity of 1.2 contains about 40 per cent. of the gas. This is very strong commercial acid. What weight could be formed by the HCl gas produced in the reaction named in the preceding problem?*

25 kilos $= .40\ x$.
$$x = \frac{25}{.40} = 62.5 \text{ kilos}.$$

6. *What is the difference between sublimation and distillation?*

A body is said to *sublime* when it rises as vapor and condenses in the solid form; when it condenses as a liquid it is said to *distil*.

7. *Why do eggs discolor silver spoons?*

The sulphur of the egg combines with the Ag, forming silver sulphide.

8. *Explain the principle of hair-dyes.*

The two principal chemicals used for dyeing the hair are lead and silver nitrate. The S in the hair combining with the Ag makes silver sulphide, or with the Pb, lead sulphide, either of which stains the hair; the former colors the skin as well as the hair, while the latter is absorbed through the skin, causing colics and other diseases such as are common among painters. The "golden yellow color" lately in fashion is produced by a solution of arsenic with the hydrosulphate of ammonia. In order to dye the lighter tints, it is necessary to bleach the hair with an alkaline solution. See *Fireside Science*, page 77.

9. *Is it safe to mix oil of vitriol and water in a glass bottle?*

The heat produced by the combination of the two will be liable to break the glass.

10. What is the color of a sulphuric acid stain on cloth? How would you remove it?

It is generally red, especially on black woolen cloth. The color may be restored by a few drops of a solution of common "soda," or ammonia.

11. What causes the milky look when oil of vitriol and water are mixed?

Pb from the stills in which the acid is condensed, and which is soluble in strong H_2SO_4, is precipitated when the acid is diluted with H_2O.

12. What is the chemical relation between animals and plants? Which perform the office of reduction, and which of oxidation?

The animal lives on *organized* materials, taking up O and evolving CO_2, and other oxidized products. The plant lives on *unorganized* materials, CO_2, HO, NH_3, and salts, organizing them and evolving O. The function of the animal is oxidation; that of the plant, reduction. The food of the plant serves merely to increase its bulk; that of the animal is employed to replace the material worn out by the active operations of life. The animal obtains the energy necessary for its existence from the oxidation of its own body; the plant obtains the energy necessary for the organization of its food directly from the sun.

13. How many pounds of S are contained in 100 lbs. of H_2SO_4?

$$S : H_2SO_4 :: x : 100 \text{ lbs.}$$
$$32 : 98 :: x : 100 \text{ lbs.}$$
$$98\,x = 3{,}200 \text{ lbs.}$$
$$x = 32\tfrac{32}{49} \text{ lbs. (S).}$$

14. How much O and H_2O are needed to change a ton of SO_3 to H_2SO_4?

One ton of SO_3 will make $1\tfrac{17}{49}$ tons of H_2SO_4: of which $\tfrac{1}{49}$ is H, $\tfrac{16}{49}$ is S, and $\tfrac{32}{49}$ is O. $\tfrac{1}{4}$ of this O, or $\tfrac{8}{49}$, comes from the air, and $\frac{1}{4} = \frac{8}{49}$ from the water. (See process of manufacture, *Chemistry*, p. 106.) Hence, $\frac{2}{49}$ (O) and $\frac{1}{49}$ (H) = $\frac{9}{49}$ of the acid, was furnished by the water—$\frac{9}{49}$ of $1\frac{17}{32}$ tons = $\frac{9}{32}$ ton (H_2O).

15. How much O in a lb. of H_2SO_4?

$\frac{32}{49}$ of any quantity of sulphuric acid are O; $\frac{1}{49}$ is H; and $\frac{16}{49}$ are S. Hence, in 1 lb. of H_2SO_2 there are $\frac{32}{49}$ lb. (O).

16. State the analogy between the compounds of O and S.

O.	S.
H_2O.	H_2S.
H_2O_2 (hydrogen dioxide).	H_2S_2.
CO_2.	CS_2.

The corresponding compounds possess not only an analogous composition, but also similar chemical properties.

148—1. In the experiment with Na_2SO_4, on page 134, an accurate thermometer will show that in making the solution, the temperature of the liquid will fall, and in its solidification, will rise. Explain.

(See *Popular Physics*, p. 250.)

Energy of temperature is absorbed in doing the work of overcoming molecular cohesion; hence, the thermometer falls while the salt is becoming liquid. In returning to the solid state it gives out this energy again as temperature.

2. If, in making a solution of Na_2SO_4, we use the salt which has effloresced, and so become anhydrous, the temperature will rise instead of falling as before. Explain.

This is because a solid hydrate is formed before the salt dissolves in the H_2O. The same holds true of other anhydrous bodies, as the chlorides of Zn, Fe, and Cu.

3. Why is KNO_3 used instead of $NaNO_3$ for making gunpowder?

Sodium nitrate is imported from Chili in large quantities, and attempts have been made to use it for making gunpowder,*

---

*Gunpowder is an intimate mechanical mixture of about 1 part niter, 1 part sulphur, and 3 parts charcoal. These proportions, however, vary but its tendency to attract moisture has frustrated the plan. It is now extensively used as a fertilizer, and is said to be the cheapest form in which N can be furnished the soil.

4. Why is a potassium salt preferable to a sodium one in glass-making?

Sodium salts give a greenish tint to the glass.

5. What is the glassy slag so plentiful about a furnace? *

A silicate of lime or some other base contained in the ore.

Ordinary Slag from Blast Furnace (Bloxam).

Silica	43.07
Alumina	14.85
Lime	28.92
Magnesia	5.87
Oxide of iron	2.53
Oxide of manganese	1.37
Potash	1.84
Sulphide of calcium	1.90
Phosphoric acid	trace
	100.35

somewhat in different countries, as well as in different sorts of powder. More charcoal adds to its power, but also causes it to attract moisture from the air, which of course injures its quality. For blasting rocks, where a sustained force, rather than an instantaneous one, is required, the powder contains more sulphur, and is even then often mixed with sawdust to retard the explosion. The niter, sulphur, and charcoal, having been ground and sifted separately, are thoroughly mixed, and then made into a thick paste with water. This is ground for some hours under edge-stones, after which it is subjected to immense pressure between gun-metal plates, forming what is known as *press-cake*. These cakes are then submitted to the action of toothed rollers, whereby the granulation of the powder is effected. The grains thus formed are sorted into different sizes by means of a series of sieves, and thoroughly dried at a steam heat. The last operation, that of polishing, is accomplished in revolving barrels, after which the powder is ready for market. The heavier the powder, the greater is its explosive power. Good powder should resist pressure between the fingers, giving no dust when rubbed, and have a slightly glossy aspect.—YOUMANS.

* The slag is commonly employed for road-making in the neighborhood of the iron-works. Some attempts have been made to turn the slag to account by employing it as a manure for soils deficient in potash, of which

6. State the formulæ of niter, saleratus, carbonate and bicarbonate of soda, plaster, pearlash, saltpeter, plaster of Paris, gypsum, carbonate and bicarbonate of potash, sal-soda, and soda.

Niter, saltpeter..KNO$_3$.
Saleratus, pearlash.....................................HKCO$_3$.
Carbonate of soda, sal-soda.........................Na$_2$CO$_3$.
Bicarbonate of soda, "soda".........................HNaCO$_3$.
Plaster, gypsum..CaSO$_4$,2H$_2$O.
Plaster of Paris...CaSO$_4$.

7. Explain how ammonium carbonate is formed in the process of making coal-gas.

Nitrogen exists in small quantities in coal, and when that is distilled at a high temperature, the elements in their nascent state combine to form this compound.

8. Upon what fact depends the formation of stalactites?

Water containing carbonic acid in solution will dissolve carbonate of lime freely, but when, on exposure to the air, the gas escapes, the carbonate is deposited.

9. Why is HF kept in gutta-percha bottles?

Because it will dissolve silica, and so destroy a glass bottle.

10. Explain the use of borax in washing.

It softens "hard" water by uniting with the soluble salts of lime or magnesia, and making insoluble ones which settle and form a thin sediment in the bottom of pitchers in which it is placed.

11. How are petrifactions formed?

Certain springs contain large quantities of some alkaline carbonate; their waters, therefore, dissolve silica abundantly. If we place a bit of wood in them, as fast as it decays, parti-

it will be seen that the above slag contains nearly $\frac{1}{6}$th of its weight, in a form which would be easily rendered available for plants by the combined action of air and moisture. When the slag is run into water, or blown into a frothy condition by the blast, it resembles pumice-stone, and is easily ground to a powder fit for applying to the soil.

cles of silica will take its place—atom by atom—and thus petrify the wood. The wood has not been *changed to* stone, but has been *replaced by* stone.

12. In what part of the body, and in what forms, is phosphorus found?

As a phosphate it is the principal earthy constituent of the bones. It is also a never-failing ingredient of the brain and nervous system. The susceptibility of phosphorus to oxidation especially adapts it to the rapid changes incident to the structure and offices of the brain.*

* Phosphorus is an element which can imperceptibly and quickly pass from a condition of great chemical activity to one of equal chemical inertness. In virtue of this character, it "may follow the blood in its changes, may oxidize in the one great set of capillaries, and be indifferent to oxygen in the other; may occur in the brain, in the vitreous form, changing as quickly as the intellect or imagination demands, and literally flaming that thoughts may breathe and words may burn; and may be present in the bones in its amorphous form, content like an impassive caryatid, to sustain upon its unwearied shoulders the mere dead weight of stones of flesh. And what is here said of the brain as contrasted with the bones, will apply with equal or similar force to many other organs of the body. All throughout the living system, we may believe that phosphorus is found at the centers of vital action in the active condition, and at its outlying points in the passive condition. In the one case it is like the soldier with his loaded musket pressed to his shoulder and his finger on the trigger, almost anticipating the command to fire; in the other it is like the same soldier with his unloaded weapon at his side standing at ease."

"Further, phosphorus forms with oxygen a powerful acid, capable even of abstracting water from sulphuric acid, and yet perfectly unirritating to the organic textures. Taking up varying quantities of water, phosphoric acid assumes no fewer than three distinct forms, which will unite with one, two, or three atoms of alkali respectively, giving an acid, neutral, or alkaline reaction. Thus it is available for the most varied uses in the body. A child is beginning to walk, and the bones of its limbs must be strengthened and hardened; phosphoric acid, accordingly, carries with it three units of lime to them, and renders them solid and firm. But the bones of its skull must remain comparatively soft and yielding, for it has many a fall, and the more elastic these bones are, the less will it suffer when its head strikes a hard object; so that in them we may suppose the phosphoric acid to retain but two units of lime, and to form a softer, less consistent solid. And the cartilages of the ribs must be still more supple and elastic, so that in them the phosphoric acid may be supposed to be

13. Why are matches poisonous? What is the antidote?

Because of the phosphorus in the match. Turpentine has been proposed as a remedy, but is not known to be reliable.

14. Will the burning phosphorus ignite the wood of the match?

It does not give off enough heat in its oxidation to raise the temperature of the wood to the igniting point. Some substance of low kindling point, such as sulphur, or which contains a large amount of O, such as $KClO_3$, is added to produce violent oxidation and kindle the wood.

15. What principle is illustrated in the ignition of a match by friction?

The conversion of motion into heat.

16. How much H_2O would be required to dissolve a pound of KNO_3?

3½ lbs. of cold water, or ⅛ lb. of hot water.

17. What causes the bad odor after the discharge of a gun?

The potassium sulphide gradually gives up its S to form H_2S.

combined with but one unit of base. On the other hand, its teeth must be harder than its hardest bones, and a new demand is made on the lime-phosphates to associate themselves with other lime-salts (especially fluoride of calcium), to form the cutting edges and grinding faces of the incisors and molars. All the while, also, the blood must be kept alkaline, that oxidation of the tissues may be promoted, and albumen retained in solution; and yet it must not be too alkaline, or tissues and albumen will both be destroyed, and the carbonic acid developed at the systemic capillaries will not be exchanged for oxygen when the blood is exposed to that gas at the lungs. So phosphoric acid provides a salt containing two units of soda and one of water, which is sufficiently alkaline to promote oxidation, dissolve albumen, and absorb carbonic acid, and yet holds the latter so loosely, that it instantly exchanges it for oxygen when it encounters that gas in the pulmonary capillaries. Again, the flesh juice must be kept acid (perhaps in opposition to the alkaline blood, as affecting the transmission of the electric currents which traverse the tissues), and phosphoric acid provides a salt, containing two units of water and one of potash, which secures the requisite acidity."—DR. G. WILSON, *Edinburgh Essays*, 1856.

18. Write in parallel columns the properties of common and of red phosphorus.

Common phosphorus.	Amorphous phosphorus.
1. Specific gravity—1.83.	1. Specific gravity—2.14.
2. Burns at 111°.	2. Burns at 500°.
3. Odor of garlic.	3. Odorless.
4. Soluble in CS_2.	4. Insoluble in CS_2.
5. Colorless, or straw-yellow.	5. Brownish red.
6. A deadly poison.	6. Harmless.

19. What causes the difference between fine and coarse salt?

(See *Chemistry*, p. 132.)

The rapidity of evaporation in the process of manufacture.

20. Why do the figures in a glass paper-weight look larger when seen from the top than from the bottom?

The form of the glass acts like a convex lens to magnify the apparent size of the figures.

21. What is the difference between water-slacked and air-slacked lime?

The former is simply calcium hydrate, CaO, H_2O, while the latter has absorbed both H_2O and CO_2 from the air.

22. Why do oyster-shells on the grate of a coal-stove prevent the formation of clinkers?

The lime of the shells acts as a flux with the iron in the coal, thus dissolving the clinkers, if any form.

23. How is lime-water made from oyster-shells?

The shells are burned, driving off the CO_2 combined with the CaO in the $CaCO_3$, and the lime thus formed is slightly soluble in water.

24. Why do newly plastered walls remain damp so long?

The plaster or mortar in drying gives off the water the lime took up in slacking.

25. Will lime lose its beneficial effect upon a soil after frequent applications?

Lime acts in various ways to improve the fertility of a soil. It corrects its acidity, aids in the decomposition of the rocky constituents, hastens the decay of the humus, and also makes the soil more porous. It does not, however, benefit the growing plant directly, but works up other materials in the soil. It therefore loses its effect after a time. The Belgian farmers have a proverb:
" Much lime and no manure,
Make farm and farmer poorer."

26. What causes plaster of Paris to harden again after being moistened?
(See *Chemistry*, p. 141.)

It recombines with water, which was driven off in the process of its manufacture.

27. What is the difference between sulphate and sulphite of lime?

The former is a compound of sulphuric acid; the latter of sulphurous acid.

28. What two classes of rays are especially abundant in the magnesium light?
(See *Popular Physics*, p. 243.)

The actinic and the luminous rays. The former are less than $\frac{1}{50000}$ of an inch in length, and produce chemical change.

29. What rare metals would become useful in the arts if the process of manufacture were cheapened?

Magnesium, aluminum, sodium, etc.

30. Why is lime placed in the bottom of a leach-tub?

The potash of the ashes is generally in the form of a carbonate, the acid neutralizing in part the strength of the alkali. The lime combines with the CO_2.

31. Is saleratus a salt of K or of Na?

It should be a carbonate of K, but, on account of its cheapness, the corresponding salt of Na is often sold instead.

32. Why will Na burst into a blaze when thrown on hot water, or put on wetted blotting paper?

The oxidation of the Na produces heat, part of which is absorbed by the cold water, over which the pellet moves rapidly about, so that the kindling point of H is not quite reached. If the water be previously heated, or if the Na is prevented from moving about, by resting it on wetted blotting paper, the H from the H_2O is quickly raised to its kindling point. It burns by taking O from the air, and its flame is colored yellow by volatilizing some of the Na while the rest is taking O from the water, and its hydrate is passing into solution.

33. Why are certain kinds of brick white?

They contain no iron, this being the substance which by its oxidation gives the color to common brick.

34. Illustrate the power of chemical affinity.

Half the crust of the earth is made up of oxides, whose constituents are held together by chemical affinity. To separate the O from these elements, with which it is united, is exceedingly difficult; so much so that the attempt is but rarely ever made.

35. Why does not a candle lowered into a jar of Cl go on burning indefinitely?

The Cl around it becomes mixed with HCl fumes, which stop the action.

181—1. Pb is softer than Fe; why is it not more malleable?

The facility with which a mass of metal can be hammered or rolled into a thin sheet without being torn, must depend partly upon its softness, and partly upon its tenacity. If it depended upon softness alone, lead should be the most malleable of ordinary metals; but, although it is easy to hammer a mass of lead into a flat plate, or to squeeze it between rollers, any attempt to reduce it to an extremely thin sheet fails, from its want of tenacity, which causes it to be worn into holes by percussion or friction. On the other hand, if malleability were entirely regulated by tenacity, iron would occupy the first place, whereas, on account of its hardness, it is the least malleable of metals in ordinary use; while gold, occupying an intermediate position with respect to tenacity, is the most malleable, which appears surprising to those who are only acquainted with gold in its ordinary forms of coin and ornament, in which it is hardened and rendered much less malleable by the presence of copper and silver.

I.—Relative Malleability of the Metals.

1. Gold.
2. Silver.
3. Copper.
4. Tin.
5. Platinum.
6. Lead.
7. Zinc.
8. Iron.

II.—Relative Tenacity of the Metals.

Lead	1	Silver	12¼
Tin	1½	Platinum	15
Zinc	2	Copper	18
Palladium	11½	Iron	27½
Gold	12	Steel	42

III.—Relative Ductility of the Metals.

1. Gold.
2. Silver.
3. Platinum.
4. Iron.
5. Copper.
6. Palladium.
7. Aluminum.
8. Zinc.
9. Tin.
10. Lead.

—BLOXAM.

2. What is the cause of the changing color often seen in the scum on standing water?

(See "Interference of Light," *Popular Physics*, p. 220.)

The thin pellicles of iron-rust on standing H_2O produce a beautiful iridescent appearance, the color changing with the thickness of the oxide. A soap-bubble exhibits in the same way a play of variegated colors according to the thickness of the film in different parts.

3. How can the spectra of the metals be obtained?

(See *Astronomy*, p. 285.)

By looking through a prism at a flame containing minute portions of the volatilized metal, and no solid particles of C.

4. Ought cannon, car-axles, etc., to be used until they break or wear out?

Cannon are condemned and recast after being fired a certain number of times, even though they show no flaw, as the jarring to which they are exposed causes the iron to take on a crystalline form, and become less fibrous and tough. A cast-iron gun of 10-inch bore or less, ought to stand 1,000 rounds; larger calibers, a smaller number.

5. Why is "chilled iron" used for safes?

The iron being cooled so instantaneously, the crystals are exceedingly small, and the metal is correspondingly harder than when cast in the ordinary way.

6. Does a blacksmith plunge his work into water merely to cool it?

The metal is harder when cooled quickly, and therefore resists wear longer.

7. What causes the white coating made when we spill water on zinc?

The oxide of zinc which is formed on the surface of the metal through the favoring influence of the water.

8. Is it well to scald pickles, make sweetmeats, or fry cakes in a brass kettle?

(See *Chemistry*, p. 161.)

9. What danger is there in the use of lead pipes? Is a lining of Zn or Sn a protection?

(See *Chemistry*, p. 162, and *Fireside Science*, p. 149.)

Zinc and tin are corroded by oxygen, though less readily than Pb, and, while their salts are poisonous, the lead is soon laid bare, and this also oxidizes.

10. Is water which has stood in a metal-lined ice-pitcher healthful?

(See *Chemistry*, p. 159.)

The dissimilar metals fastened with solder, which corrodes in the presence of water, develop a voltaic current which hastens the oxidation. The salts thus formed are very dangerous.

11. If you ask for "cobalt" at a drug-store, what will you get? If for "arsenic"?

Impure metallic arsenic is sold as "cobalt," while arsenious anhydride is called "arsenic."

12. What two elements are fluid at ordinary temperatures?

Bromine and mercury.

13. Should we touch a gold ring to mercury?

The mercury will form with the gold an amalgam.

14. Why does silver blacken if handled?

The perspiration of the body contains S, which combining with the metal forms silver sulphide, which is black.

15. Why does silver tarnish rapidly where coal is used for fires?

S, which is present in coal, forms a silver sulphide.

16. Why is a solution of coin blue?

From the Cu which is contained in silver coin forming Cu $(NO_3)_2$, which is blue.

17. Why will a solution of silver nitrate curdle brine?

A white, curdy precipitate of silver chloride is formed.

18. Why does writing with indelible ink turn black when exposed to the sun, or to a hot iron?

By the decomposition of the silver salt contained in the ink, and consequent production of Ag_2O, which stains organic matter black.

19. What alloys resemble gold?

Oroide, aluminum-bronze, etc.

20. Why does a fish-hook "rust out" the line to which it is fastened?

Ferric oxide and ferric hydrate act as conveyers of O, absorbing it from the air and giving it up to organic bodies with which they are in contact.

21. Why do the nails in clap-boards loosen?

See Question 20.

22. Show that the earth's crust is mainly composed of burnt metals. (See Cooke's *Religion and Chemistry*.)

It consists largely of potassium, magnesium, calcium, aluminum, sodium, etc., in combination with O. These compounds are the products of combustion.

The elements O, Si, Al, Mg, Ca, K, Na, Fe, C, S, H, Cl, and N—13 in all—probably make up $\frac{99}{100}$ of the earth's crust.

23. What kind of iron is used for a magnet? For a magnetic needle?

Steel for a permanent magnet, and therefore for a magnetic needle; pure soft iron for an electro-magnet.

24. Why does a "tin" pail so quickly rust out when once the tin is worn through?

These pails are made of sheet iron, which is covered with a coating of tin, which causes the popular name for them. If this is scratched through, the iron and tin in contact are exposed to the water; voltaic action is started, and the iron rapidly rusts.

25. Why is the zinc oxide found in New Jersey red, when zinc rust is white?

The oxide in New Jersey is colored by compounds of iron and manganese.

26. Should we filter a solution of permanganate of potash through paper? (See *Chemistry*, p. 157, note.)

No. The salt will give up O and corrode the filter.

27. Why is wood, cordage, etc., sometimes soaked in a solution of corrosive sublimate?

This salt possesses strong antiseptic properties.

28. Why does the white paint around a sink turn black?

H_2S is set free, which, acting on the paint, forms lead sulphide, which is black.

29. Why is aluminum, rather than platinum, used for making the smallest weights?

Because of its low specific gravity as compared with that of platinum.

30. How would you detect the presence of iron particles in black sand?

By a magnet.

31. Which metals can be welded?

Iron and platinum, most easily; others also by using a powerful electric current to heat the ends of the pieces of metal.

32. When the glassy slag from a blast-furnace has a dark color, what does it show?

It might be anticipated that the appearance of the slag would convey to the experienced eye some useful information with respect to the character of the ore and the general progress of the smelting operation. A good slag is liquid, nearly transparent, of a light-gray color, and has a fracture somewhat resembling that of limestone. A dark slag shows that much of the oxide of iron is escaping unreduced. Streaks of blue are commonly found when ores containing sulphur are being smelted, possibly from the presence of a substance similar to ultramarine, the constituents of which are all present in the slag. Again, the slags obtained in smelting ores containing titanium generally present a peculiar blistered appearance.— BLOXAM.

33. In welding iron the surfaces to be joined are sometimes sprinkled with sand. Explain.

The silica acts as a flux with the oxide upon the surface, and lays bare the metal for welding.

34. What is the difference between an alloy and an amalgam?

An amalgam is composed of mercury and some other metal. An alloy consists of any metals whatever.

35. Steel articles are blued to protect from rusting, by heating in a sand-bath. Explain.

A thin coating of oxide is formed on the surface of the metal.

36. Give the formulas for copperas and white lead.

1. $FeSO_4 = FeO,SO_3$.
2. $PbCO_3 = PbO,CO_2$.

37. Why is Hg used for filling thermometers?

Because it is fluid at all ordinary temperatures.

38. What oxides are formed by the combustion of Na, K, Zn, S, Fe, Pb, Cu, P, etc.? Which are bases? Anhydrides? Give the common name of each.

(1.) Na_2O is formed when Na oxidizes in dry air, or oxygen at a low temperature. This takes up water with great avidity, forming HNaO (NaHO), sodium hydroxide. Na_2O_2 is made when Na is heated to 200° C. HNaO is the caustic soda of commerce, and is an alkaline base.

(2.) K in a similar manner, depending upon the temperature, forms K_2O, K_2O_2, and K_2O_4. The first, with water, forms the ordinary caustic potash, HKO, of commerce. It is an alkaline base.

(3.) ZnO is the only known oxide of zinc. It forms salts.

(4.) Seven compounds of S and O are known, but only two are of interest—the familiar anhydrides, SO_2 and SO_3.

(5.) The oxides of iron are four in number: (1) the monoxide, or ferrous oxide, FeO, from which the green ferrous salts are derived; (2) the sesquioxide, or ferric oxide, Fe_2O_3, yielding the yellow ferric salts; (3) the magnetic or black oxide, Fe_3O_4, which does not form any definite salts; (4) ferric acid, H_2FeO_4, a weak acid, forming colored salts with potassium.

(6.) Pb forms two oxides, the monoxide and the dioxide. The former is the well-known litharge, which is the base of the lead salts.

(7.) Cu has two oxides—the cuprous (Cu_2O) and cupric (CuO), both of which form salts, thus giving rise to two series, the cuprous and the cupric salts. The two oxides are commonly known as the red and the black.

(8.) Phosphorus forms two oxides, phosphorous anhydride (P_2O_3) and phosphoric anhydride (P_2O_5).

39. Is charcoal lighter than H_2O?

Charcoal appears at first sight to be lighter than water, as a piece of it floats on the surface of this liquid; this is, however, due to the porous nature of the charcoal, for if it be finely powdered it sinks to the bottom of the water.—ROSCOE.

40. Name the vitriols.

The compounds of sulphuric acid, commonly called "the vitriols," are as follows:

    1. Sulphate of iron, Green vitriol.
    2. Sulphate of copper, Blue vitriol.
    3. Sulphate of zinc, White vitriol.

41. Is Mg univalent or bivalent? Zn?

Mg belongs to the zinc class of metals which comprises magnesium, zinc, cadmium, and indium. These are all bivalent.

42. Name some dibasic acid.

Sulphuric acid.

43. Name a neutral salt. An acid salt.

Sodium sulphate is neutral (Na_2SO_4). Hydro-sodium sulphate is acid ($HNaSO_4$).

44. Calculate the percentage of water contained in crystallized copper sulphate. Sodium sulphate. Calcium sulphate. Alum.

$$(1.)\ CuSO_4,\ 5H_2O = 249.5.$$
$$5H_2O = 90.$$

Hence, $\frac{90}{249.5} = .36 = 36\ \%$ of copper sulphate is water.

$$(2.)\ Na_2SO_4,\ 10H_2O = 322.$$
$$10H_2O = 180.$$

Hence, $\frac{180}{322} = .55 = 55\ \%$ of sodium sulphate is water.

(3.) $CaSO_4, 2H_2O = 172$.
$2H_2O = 36$.

Hence, $\frac{36}{172} = .20 = 20\%$ of gypsum is water.

(4.) $Al_2K_2, 4SO_4 + 24H_2O = 949$.
$24H_2O = 432$.

Hence, $\frac{432}{949} = .45 = 45\%$ of potash alum is water.

45. What is the test for Ag? Cu?

Ag can be easily detected when in solution by the precipitation of the white, curdy chloride, insoluble in H_2O and HNO_3, and soluble in H_3N: the metal can be obtained in malleable globules before the blowpipe, and is reduced from its solutions by Fe, Cu, P, and Hg. Ag is estimated quantitatively either as the chloride or as the metal.

Copper may be tested (1) by the black insoluble sulphide; (2) by the blue hydrate turning black on heating; (3) by the deep-blue coloration with ammonia; (4) by the deposition of red metallic copper upon a bright surface of iron placed in the solution.

46. What weight of crystallized "tin salts" ($SnCl_2$, $2H_2O$) can be prepared from one ton of metallic tin?

$Sn : SnCl_2, 2H_2O :: 2,000$ lbs. $: x$.
$118 : \quad 225 \quad :: 2,000$ lbs. $: x$.
$118 \, x = 450,000$ lbs.
$x = 3813.56$ lbs. ($SnCl_2, 2H_2O$).

47. 100 parts by weight of silver yield 132.87 parts of silver chloride. Given the atomic weight of chlorine (35.4), required that of silver.

$32.87 : 100 :: 35.4 : x$.
$x = 108+$.

48. What is the composition of slacked lime?

(See *Chemistry*, p. 139.)

CaO, H_2O.

49. How is ferrous sulphate obtained? How many tons of crystals can be obtained by the slow oxidation of

230 tons of iron pyrites containing 37.5 per cent. of sulphur?
(See *Chemistry*, p. 158.)

$37\frac{1}{2}$ % of 230 = 86.25 tons, the weight of S contained in the pyrites.

$$S : FeSO_4, 7H_2O :: 86.25 : x.$$
$$32 : \quad 278 \quad :: 86.25 : x.$$
$$x = 749.296 \text{ tons of } FeSO_4, 7H_2O.$$

50. *Required 500 tons of soda crystals; what will be the weight of salt and pure sulphuric acid needed?*

Find (1) how much Na there is in 500 tons of "soda," and (2) how much NaCl would be needed to furnish that amount of the metal in case all were utilized.

$$(1.) \ Na_2 : Na_2CO_3, 10H_2O :: x : 500 \text{ tons.}$$
$$46 : \quad 286 \quad :: x : 500 \text{ tons.}$$
$$286 \ x = 23,000 \text{ tons.}$$
$$x = 80.42 - \text{tons (Na).}$$

(2.) $\frac{2 3 0}{5 8 5}$ of any amount of NaCl is Na; hence, to furnish 80.42 tons of Na would require $\frac{5 8 5}{2 3 0} \times 80.42$ tons = 204.546 tons (NaCl).

(3.) By comparing the atomic weights of the substances, it will be seen that for 46 parts of Na there must be 98 of pure H_2SO_4. $\frac{9 8}{4 6} \times 204.546$ tons = 435.771 tons (H_2SO_4).

51. *Describe the uses of lime in agriculture.*

Lime acts in various ways to improve the fertility of a soil. It corrects its acidity, aids in the decomposition of the rocky constituents, hastens the decay of the humus, and also makes the soil more porous. It does not, however, benefit the growing plant directly, but works up other materials in the soil. It therefore loses its effect after a time.

52. *How many tons of oil of vitriol, containing 70 per cent. of pure acid (H_2SO_4), can be prepared from 250 tons of iron pyrites, containing 42 per cent. of sulphur?*

(1.) (See Question 49.) 250 tons × .42 = 105 tons (S).

$$(2.) \ S : H_2SO_4 :: 105 \text{ tons} : x.$$
$$32 : \ 98 \ :: 105 \text{ tons} : x.$$
$$32 \ x = 10,290 \text{ tons.}$$
$$x = 321.56 \text{ tons } (H_2SO_4).$$

(3.) If 321.56 tons (H_2SO_4) is 70 % of the given oil of vitriol, the entire amount would be 321.56 tons $\times \frac{100}{70} = 459.28$ tons (oil of vitriol).

247—1. *How would you prove the presence of tannin in tea?*

By adding a few drops of a solution of ferrous sulphate. This would form a dark precipitate of iron tannate.

2. *How would you test for Fe in a solution?*
(See Miller's *Inorganic Chemistry*, p. 525.)

A solution of nutgalls will give a bluish-black, inky precipitate. The ferrous- or proto-salts are distinguished by their light green color, and by their solutions giving (1) a white precipitate, with caustic alkalies; (2) a light blue precipitate, with potassium ferrocyanide, which rapidly becomes dark; while the ferric- or per-salts are yellow-colored, and their solutions yield (1) a deep reddish-brown precipitate, with the caustic alkalies; and (2) a deep-blue precipitate (Prussian blue), with potassium ferrocyanide.

3. *Why can we settle coffee with an egg?*

The albumen of the egg coagulates by heat, and, entangling the particles of coffee, mechanically carries them to the bottom.

4. *How would you show the presence of starch in a potato?*

A solution of iodine will form the blue iodide of starch.

5. *Why is starch stored in the seed of a plant?*

For the growth of the young plant.

6. *Why are unbleached cotton goods dark-colored?*

Because of the dirt gathered in the process of manufacture. The cotton balls are snowy white.

7. *Why do beans, rice, etc., swell when cooked?*

On account of the bursting of the starch granules.

8. *Why does decaying wood darken?*

On account of the formation of humus, which contains carbon in excess.

9. How would you show that C exists in sugar?
By heating it until the H and O are all driven off. A mass of porous charcoal remains on the plate.

10. Why do fruits lose their sweetness when over-ripe?
(See Miller's *Organic Chemistry*, p. 875.)
The vegetable acid contained in the fruit when green, oxidizes as the ripening process continues, O being absorbed, and CO_2 evolved. If this continues too long, the sugar itself becomes oxidized.

11. Why does maple-sap lose its sweetness when the leaf starts?
The sugar of the sap is applied to the wants of the growing tree.

12. Should yeast-cakes be allowed to freeze?
A cold of 32° will kill the ferment.

13. Why will wine sour if the bottle be not well corked?
The presence of air will cause the continuation of the oxidizing process into the second or acetic stage.

14. Why can vinegar be made from sweetened water and brown paper?
The paper acts as a ferment, while the sugar or molasses is oxidized into alcohol, and thence into acetic acid.

15. Why should the vinegar-barrel be kept in a warm place?
Fermentation takes place to the best advantage at a special temperature, about 70° F.

16. Why does "scalding" check the "working" of preserves?
The ferment which causes the fermentation is killed by the heat.

17. Is the oxalic acid in the pie-plant poisonous?

It is neutralized by the alkaline base, with which it is combined in the plant.

18. How may ink-stains be removed?

By a solution of oxalic acid, forming an iron oxalate which is soluble in water, and hence may be washed out.

19. Why is leather black on only one side?

The solution of copperas, which blackens the leather, is applied on only one side.

20. Why do drops of tea stain a knife-blade?

The tannic acid of the tea combines with the iron, forming an iron tannate.*

21. Why will not coffee stain it in the same way?
(See Miller's *Organic Chemistry*, p. 549.)

The modification of tannin contained in coffee, unlike that in tea, turns a solution of ferrous sulphate green, and will not precipitate one of gelatin.

22. Why does writing-fluid darken on exposure to the air?

It absorbs O, the iron changing to ferric oxide.

23. What causes the disagreeable smell of a smoldering wick?

A volatile substance, termed acrolein, is produced in the decomposition of the oil.

24. Why does ink corrode steel pens?

The free sulphuric acid of the ink combines with the iron of the pen.

---

* The tannic acid of the tea tans the albumen of the milk used in seasoning the tea, forming flakes of real leather. It has been calculated that an average tea-drinker, in this way, makes and drinks enough leather each year to make a pair of shoes. The albumen of milk uniting with the tannic acid of tea, softens its flavor. This is generally preferred to the harsh, clear beverage.

25. How does a bird obtain the $CaCO_3$ for its egg shells?
(See chemistry of a hen's egg in *Fireside Science*.)

A common hen's egg is 95 per cent. carbonate of lime, one per cent. phosphate of lime and magnesia, and two per cent. animal matter. The shell would weigh over 100 grains, so that a hen laying 100 eggs in a season would require nearly 1¼ lbs. of $CaCO_3$. The hen must in part secrete this from her food, and in part gather it from the sand, pebbles, etc., she picks up amid her incessant scratching and searching.

26. Why does new soap act on the hands more than old?

The spent lye, which contains the excess of alkali, gradually separates from the soap, leaving only the salts in which the alkali is neutralized by the fatty acids. Also a more complete combination takes place, whereby some free alkali is taken up by the acids, perhaps before uncombined. The former statement is especially true in the case of soft or home-made soap.

27. What is the shiny coat on certain leaves and fruits?
A species of wax secreted by the plant.

28. Why does turpentine burn with so much smoke?
Because it contains an excess of carbon.

29. Why is the nozzle of a turpentine bottle so sticky?

The turpentine on exposure to the air oxidizes, turning to rosin.

30. Why does kerosene give more light than alcohol?

It contains more carbon, which, when heated in the flame of the burning H, gives out a white light.

31. What is the antidote to oxalic acid? Why?
Magnesia or chalk, forming an insoluble oxalate.

32. Would you weaken camphor spirits with water?

No; since camphor is insoluble in dilute alcohol. The principle is the same as that of the precipitation of lead from dilute sulphuric acid.

33. What is the difference between rosin and resin?

Rosin is an oxidized resin. Rosin is a species, and resin a genus.

34. Why does skim-milk look blue and new milk white?

The globules of butter contained in new milk reflect the light, and so make it look white; but when they are removed, by the separation of the cream, more light is transmitted, and only the blue is reflected to the eye.

35. Why does an ink-spot turn yellow after washing with soap?

The free alkali of the soap combines with the tannic acid of the ink, leaving the oxide of iron (ferric oxide), which stains the cloth yellow.

ANSWERS

TO THE

PRACTICAL QUESTIONS

IN THE

NEW DESCRIPTIVE ASTRONOMY.

32.—*1. How high is the North Star above your horizon?*
(See *Astronomy*, p. 218.)

It should be remembered that the North Star revolves around the true North Pole at a distance of about 1¼°; hence it marks the exact height of the Pole above the horizon only twice in twenty-four hours.

2. What is the sun's right ascension at the autumnal equinox? At the vernal equinox?

At the vernal equinox, the sun is in Aries, and its R. A.=0. At the autumnal equinox, it is in Libra, and its R. A.=180°.

3. What was the first discovery made by the telescope?
(See *Astronomy*, p. 20; articles in Appletons' *Cyclopedia* on Telescope and Galileo; and, also, Routledge's *History of Science*, p. 107.)

Galileo's telescope was constructed on the principle of an opera-glass.

4. How high above the horizon of any place are the equinoctial points when they pass the meridian?
(See *Astronomy*, note, p. 27.)

The co-latitude of the place.

5. Jupiter revolves around the sun in 12 of our years. Assuming the earth's distance from the sun to be 93,000,000 miles, compute Jupiter's distance by applying Kepler's third law.
(See *Astronomy*, note, p. 19.)

If we square the period of any planet, expressed in years, and extract the cube root of this product, the result will be the mean distance from the sun, expressed in astronomical units, *i.e.*, in radii of the earth's orbit. Jupiter's period of 12 years will give a result of 5.2028. 93,000,000 miles × 5.2028 = 483,-860,400 miles.

6. *The latitude of Albany is 42° 39′ N.; what is the sun's meridian altitude at that place when it is in the celestial equator?*

(See *Astronomy*, note, p. 27.)

90° − 42° 39′ = 47° 21′.

7. *What is the co-latitude of a place?*

(See *Astronomy*, note, p. 27.)

The co-latitude is the complement of the latitude.

8. *What is the declination of the zenith of the place in which you reside?*

(See *Astronomy*, note, p. 27.)

It equals the latitude.

9. *Why are the stars generally invisible by day?*

(See *Astronomy*, p. 25.)

The stars would be visible in the day-time if it were not for the atmosphere. Compare the description of a lunar sky, on page 134 of the *Astronomy*.

10. *Why is the ecliptic so called?*

(See *Astronomy*, note, p. 58.)

11. *Who first taught that the earth is round?*

The discovery of the rotundity of the earth has been ascribed to Thales; others attribute it to Aristotle.

12. *What is Astrology?*

A magic art that pretends to foretell events by means of the stars.

13. *How can we distinguish the fixed stars from the planets?*

(See *Astronomy*, pp. 2 and 203.)

14. How long was the Ptolemaic system accepted?

It was taught in the schools for about 1400 years, or until the time of Galileo—the 17th century.

15. In what respect did the Copernican system differ from the one now received?
(See *Astronomy*, p. 14.)

16. For what is Astronomy indebted to Galileo? To Newton?

Galileo discovered the structure of the moon; the existence of Jupiter's moons and their revolution around their primary; the stars of the milky way; and the rotation of the sun on its axis (as proved by the appearance of the spots). Newton discovered the law of gravitation, and by means of it explained the specific gravity of the planets, the cause of the tides, the shape of the earth, the theory of precession of the equinoxes, and the paths of the comets. Read Brewster's *Life of Newton;* also, Buckley's *History of Natural Science.*

17. What is the amount of the obliquity of the ecliptic?
(See *Astronomy*, p. 29.)

18. Define Zenith. Nadir. Azimuth. Altitude. Equinoctial. Right Ascension. Declination. Equinox. Ecliptic. Colure. Solstice. Polar distance. Zenith distance. The Zodiac.

These terms are defined under the various subjects on pp. 26-30 of the *Astronomy.*

19. If the R. A. of the sun be 80°, state in what sign he is then located. 160°. 280°.
(See *Astronomy*, table on p. 31.)

1 sign = 30°. 80° would locate the sun in Gemini; 160°, in Virgo; 280°, in Capricornus.

20. Why does the angle which the ecliptic makes with the horizon vary?
(See *Astronomy*, p. 29.)

The angle between the horizon and the celestial equator is constant; the ecliptic being oblique to the equator, the angle that it makes with the horizon must vary as it revolves.

21. Why is the angle which the celestial equator makes with the horizon constant?

(See *Astronomy*, p. 29.)

The celestial equator is perpendicular to the axis of the heavens, and hence all parts of it make the same angle with the celestial axis and with the horizon.

198—1. Would the earth rise and set to a Lunarian?

(See *Astronomy*, p. 134.)

The earth would not rise or set, as the moon does with us, but would merely oscillate to and fro through a few degrees. A Lunarian would see the earth constantly in the sky, undergoing all the phases the moon presents to the earth. But when it is full moon to us, it is new earth on the moon. During the first and last quarters, the changes would occur during the daytime; during the second and third, in the night. The rapid rotation of the earth, repeated fifteen times during a lunar night, must greatly diversify the appearance of the earth.—See Olmstead's *Letters on Astronomy*, p. 180.

2. Could there be a transit of Jupiter?

(See *Astronomy*, p. 67.)

No. Jupiter is a superior planet.

3. Why does Mars' inner-moon rise in the west?

(See *Astronomy*, note on p. 153.)

This satellite performs a revolution in its orbit in less than half the time that Mars revolves on its axis. In consequence, to the inhabitants of Mars, it would seem to rise in the west and set in the east. The revolution of the moon around the earth and of the earth on its axis, are both from west to east; but, the latter revolution being the more rapid, the apparent diurnal motion of the moon is from east to west. In the case of the inner satellite of Mars, however, this is reversed, and it therefore appears to move in the actual direction of its orbital motion. The rapidity of its phases is also equally remarkable. It is less than two hours from new moon to first quarter.—Newcomb and Holden's *Astronomy*, p. 339.

4. In what part of the sky do you always look for the planets?

Within the limits of the Zodiac. A few of the asteroids only pass outside this belt of the heavens.

5. Show how it was impossible for the darkness that occurred at the time of the Crucifixion of Christ to have been caused by an eclipse of the sun.

The Feast of the Passover took place at full moon. "With the Jews, a month began when the new moon was seen. Persons were appointed to watch, about the time it was expected, on the tops of mountains. As soon as they saw its light, they gave notice by sounding trumpets and building fires."—Nevin's *Biblical Antiquities*.

6. Is there any danger of a collision between the earth and a comet?
(See *Astronomy*, p 192.)

A collision between the earth and a comet must be a rare occurrence. Babinet computed that one would strike the earth, on the average, every 15,000,000 years. There are certainly, however, comets whose orbits cross the earth's path, and if we should happen to reach the crossing at the same time with one of them, there would be a collision. We should probably never know of the event unless we were watching for it.

7. How are aerolites distinguished?
(See *Astronomy*, pp. 177, 178.)

Aerolites, when found, generally have an exterior crust of fused material, presenting a glossy, pitch-like appearance. An analysis of the interior commonly presents a combination of elements that is so characteristic as to identify the body as an aerolite even when not seen to fall. Large masses have been found in Northern Mexico which are thus known to be of meteoric origin.

"The meteoric stones may be divided into two distinct groups—*meteoric iron*, and *meteoric stones proper*.

"1. Meteoric iron is an alloy of iron and nickel, containing about 10 per cent. of nickel, and small quantities of cobalt, manganese, magnesium, tin, copper, and carbon. This alloy has not been found among terrestrial minerals.

" 2. The meteoric stones proper are composed of minerals of volcanic origin, and such as are found abundantly in terrestrial lavas and trap-rocks, viz. :

Magnetic iron,	Olivine,
Sphene,	Anorthite,
Chrome iron,	Labradorite,
Apatite (?),	Augite,

together with a varying proportion of the meteoric iron-nickel alloy."—Haughton's *Astronomy*.

8. When do we see the old moon in the west after sunrise?
(See *Astronomy*, p. 127.)

9. When do we see the moon high in the eastern sky in the afternoon before the sun sets?
(See *Astronomy*, p. 127.)

During the second quarter, before she comes into opposition.

10. When is a planet morning, and when evening, star?
(See *Astronomy*, pp. 65, 70.)

11. Is the sun really hotter in summer than in winter?
(See *Astronomy*, p. 101.)

12. Why is a planet invisible at conjunction?
(See *Astronomy*, p. 65.)

13. Must an inferior planet always be in the same part of the sky as the sun? A superior planet?
(See *Astronomy*, pp. 64 and 67.)

14. Why, in summer, does the sun, at rising and at setting, shine on the north side of certain houses?

Since at the summer solstice the sun rises and sets north of the E. and W. points, it will rise and set on the north side of a house which stands exactly N. and S. At the winter solstice the sun rises and sets S. of the E. and W. points.

15. What effect does the volume of a planet have upon the force of gravity at its surface?
(See *Astronomy*, pp. 40, 80.)

16. In what part of the heavens do we see the new moon? The old moon? The crescent moon?
(See *Astronomy*, p. 127 et seq.)

It is a very interesting experiment to notice how soon after conjunction we can observe the new moon. Observers have detected her when twenty-three hours old, and an instance is on record of the moon's thin crescent being seen early one morning before sunrise, and after sundown the following day.

17. What is the Golden Number in the almanac?
(See *Astronomy*, p. 145.)

18. Why do we have more lunar than solar eclipses?
(See *Astronomy*, p. 146.)

Really, solar eclipses occur more frequently than lunar eclipses, but the latter are oftener seen at any particular place, because they are visible over a larger area of territory on the earth.

19. In what direction do the horns of the moon turn?
(See *Astronomy*, p. 127.)

20. Is the "tidal wave" a progressive movement of the water?
(See *Astronomy*, note, p. 148.)

The wind raises the particles of water, and gravity draws them back again. They thus vibrate up and down, but do not advance. The forward movement of the wave is an illusion. The *form* of the wave progresses, but not the water of which it is composed, any more than the thread of the screw which we turn in our hand, or the undulations of a rope or carpet which is shaken, or the stalks of grain which bend in billows as the wind sweeps over them. Near the shore the oscillations are shorter, and the waves, unbalanced by the deep water, are forced forward till the lower part of each one is checked by the friction on the sandy beach, the front becomes well-nigh vertical, and the upper part curls over and falls beyond.

21. Why does the sun "cross the line" in some years on March 21, and, in others, on March 22?
(See *Astronomy*, p. 99.)

Leap-year also throws the dates back one day.

22. Do we ever see the sun where it really is?
(See *Astronomy*, p. 114.)

Both refraction and aberration of light change the apparent place of the sun.

23. "At Edinburgh, Scotland, there are times when the sun rises at 3¼ o'clock A.M., and sets at 8¼ o'clock P.M., and the twilight lasts the entire night." When and why is this?
(See *Astronomy*, p. 116.)

The latitude of Edinburgh is 55° 57'. Any place north of 48° 33' will have twilight at midnight in midsummer; for 90° − 23° 27' (the sun's declination) − 18° (at which twilight ceases) = 48° 33'. The hours named in the problem are the times for the rising and setting of the sun at Edinburgh at the summer solstice.

24. Which is the longest day of the year?
(See *Astronomy*, p. 99.)

The summer solstice points out the longest day of the year.

25. Is the moon nearer to us when it is at the horizon, or at the zenith?
(See *Astronomy*, p. 124.)

The moon is nearer to us when it is at the zenith than when it is at the horizon.

26. How many solar eclipses would happen each year if the orbits of the sun and the moon were in the same plane?
(See *Astronomy*, p. 138.)

In that case a solar eclipse would occur every new moon.

27. Is there any heat in moonlight?
(See *Astronomy*, p. 125.)

28. Can we see the moon during a total eclipse?
(See *Astronomy*, p. 146.)

29. Which of the planets are repeating a portion of the earth's history?

Spectrum Analysis renders it possible, perhaps probable, that Jupiter and Saturn, and, may be, Uranus and Neptune, have not yet attained that degree of density which must necessarily precede the formation of a solid surface. They are, therefore, now in a geologic age similar to that in which the earth existed before its crust had become solidified. (See Schellen's *Spectrum Analysis*, p. 337.)

30. How many times does the moon turn on her axis each year?
(See *Astronomy*, p. 123.)

The moon turns on her axis once each month.

31. Can you explain the different signs used in the almanac?
(See "Astronomical Signs" in the Dictionary.)

32. Show how the moon is a prophecy of the earth's future.

The moon is a worn-out globe, and presents the same appearance that the earth will probably offer ages hence.

33. Does the sun really rise and set?
(See *Astronomy*, pp. 14, 87.)

No. This is only an optical illusion, being an illustration of our tendency to transfer motion.

34. Are the bright portions of the moon mountains or plains?

The lofty portions, or mountains, of the moon reflect the light to the earth most strongly, and hence appear the brightest. The deep valleys, lying in shadow, look dark.

35. Which of the heavenly bodies are self-luminous?
(See above, Question 29; also *Astronomy*, note, p. 163.)

Jupiter and Saturn probably emit light, at least from the brighter spots of their surface. Read Newcomb's *Astronomy*, p. 342.

36. Why is not a solar eclipse visible over the whole earth?
(See *Astronomy*, p. 140.)

37. What is meant by the "mean distance" of a planet?

The "mean distance" is the average distance.

38. What keeps the earth in motion around the sun?
(See *Astronomy*, p. 22.)

According to the First Law of Motion, "Every body continues in its state of rest or of uniform motion in a straight line, except in so far as it may be compelled by impressed forces to change that state."

39. Do we ever see the sun after it sets?
(See *Astronomy*, p. 114.)

The refraction of the atmosphere tends to raise all objects toward the zenith, and, at the horizon, this is no less than 35', or 3' more than the mean diameter of the sun (32').

40. When does the earth move the most rapidly in its orbit?
(See *Astronomy*, p. 18.)

The earth moves most rapidly in perihelion.

41. Have we conclusive evidence that any planet is inhabited?
(See *Astronomy*, p. 61; also note, p. 207.)

May it not be that the same lavish hand that scatters flowers and seeds in such profusion (not one in a thousand coming to the perfection and end of its being), sows space with worlds, a few only reaching the full fruition of life?

42. When is twilight the longest? The shortest? Why?
(See *Astronomy*, p. 116.)

Twilight is usually reckoned to last until the sun's depression below the horizon amounts to 18°; this, however, varies; in the tropics a depression of 16° or 17° is sufficient to put an end to the phenomenon, but in England a depression of 17° to 21° is required. The duration of twilight differs in different latitudes; it varies also in the same latitude at different seasons of the year, and depends, in some measure, on the meteorological condition of the atmosphere. Strictly speaking, in the latitude of Greenwich there is no true night from May 22 to July 21, but constant twilight from sunset to sunrise. Twilight reaches its minimum three weeks before the vernal equinox, and three weeks after the autumnal equinox, when its duration is 1 hr. 50 min. At midwinter it is longer by about seventeen minutes; but the augmentation is frequently not perceptible, owing to the greater prevalence of clouds and haze at that season of the year, which intercept the light, and hinder it from reaching the earth. The duration is least at the equator (1 hr. 12 min.), and increases as we approach the poles; for at the former there are two twilights every twenty-four hours, but at the latter only two in a year, each lasting about fifty days. At the north pole the sun is below the horizon for six months, but from January 29 to the vernal equinox, and from the autumnal equinox to November 12, the sun is less than 18° below the horizon; so that there is twilight during the whole of these intervals, and thus the length of the actual night is reduced to $2\frac{1}{2}$ months. The length of the day in these regions is about six months, during the whole of which time the sun is constantly above the horizon. The general rule is, *that to the inhabitants of an oblique sphere the twilight is longer in proportion as the place is nearer the elevated pole, and the sun is farther from the equator on the side of the elevated pole.—Chambers' Astronomy.*

When the sun rises or sets most obliquely to the horizon, then the least time is required to pass through the necessary 18°, and, of course, the length of twilight is the least. When the sun rises or sets least obliquely, the most time is required to pass through 18°, and the length of twilight is greatest. If the sun's path is perpendicular to the horizon, the sun will pass over the 18° in 1 hr. 12 min.; for 15°= 1 hr.; and hence 18°= $1\frac{3}{15}$ hr.

43. *What is a moon?*

A moon is a secondary body, or satellite, revolving about a primary body, or planet.

44. *To a person in the south temperate zone, where would the sun be at noon?*

On the meridian north of the observer.

45. *Is it correct to say that the moon revolves about the earth, when we know that, according to the law of Phys-*

ics, they must both revolve about their common center of gravity?

(See *Astronomy*, note, p. 200.)

The earth is not stationary as regards the moon, for both it and our satellite revolve together about their common center of gravity. Again, it is not the earth alone which revolves about the sun in the elliptical orbit, but this common center of gravity. The sun, also, is not stationary, but it and the planets revolve about the common center of gravity of the whole system.

46. *During a transit of Venus, do we see the body of the planet itself on the face of the sun?*

(See *Astronomy*, p. 277.)

During a transit, Venus appears as "a perfectly round *black* spot on the disk of the sun." The planet turns its unillumined side toward us, and is, strictly speaking, invisible.

47. *How many real motions has the sun? How many apparent ones?*

It has two real motions: one around its axis, and one with the solar system around the Pleiades. It has three apparent motions: one along the ecliptic,—its yearly motion; one through the heavens,—its daily motion; and one north and south.

48. *How many real motions has the earth?*

Three. One on its axis; one around the sun; and a third,— its "wabbling motion," which causes Precession.

49. *Can an inferior planet have an elongation of 90°?*

No. Venus recedes only 48° from the sun.

50. *How do we know the intensity of the sun's light on the surface of any of the planets?*

The intensity of the heat and light varies inversely as the square of the distance.

51. *Why is the Tropic of Cancer placed where it is?*

Because it is the farthest place north where the sun is ever seen directly overhead.

52. What planets would float in water?

According to Chambers' *Astronomy*, the density of Saturn is .68 that of water; Uranus, .99; Neptune, .96. According to Newcomb, Saturn's density is .75.

53. How must the moons of Jupiter appear during their transit across the disk of that planet?

The satellites appear on the disk of their primary as round luminous spots, preceded or followed by their shadows, which show as round black or blackish spots.—CHAMBERS.

54. " The shadow of the satellite precedes the satellite itself when Jupiter is passing from conjunction to opposition, but follows it between opposition and conjunction." Explain.

When actually in conjunction, the shadow is in a right line with the satellite, and the two may be superposed.

55. What facts point to the conclusion that Mars may, perhaps, have passed his planetary prime?

The proportion of land and water, and the appearance of the seas, all point to a conclusion somewhat similar to the one stated in the following quotation :

"Mars' orbit being outside the earth's, he was probably formed earlier. The mass of Mars is not much more than $\frac{1}{8}$ the earth's, and the surface about $\frac{1}{4}$; if he possessed the same degree of heat as the earth, he would have only $\frac{1}{8}$ the amount to radiate, and the supply would not last so long. Though having only $\frac{1}{4}$ the surface of the earth, he would still cool off 3 times as rapidly as the earth. Mars must, therefore, be at least three times as far on the way toward planetary decrepitude and death as our earth."—*Proctor's Poetry of Astronomy.*

56. Why may we conceive that Saturn and Jupiter are yet in their planetary youth?

(See *Astronomy*, note, p. 163.)

Vast planets, like Saturn and Jupiter, must have required for cooling a far longer time than the earth, and thus the various stages of development would occupy a much greater length of time. (Read Proctor's "When the Sea was Young," in *Poetry of Science*.)

57. Show how, if the Nebular Hypothesis be accepted, the fashioning of a planet must require an enormous length of time.
(See *Astronomy*, p. 255.)

The experiments of Bischof upon basalt show that the earth would require 350 millions of years to cool down from 2,000° C to 200° C. This enormous period would represent only one stage in the process of the earth's development. (Read Winchell's *World Life*.)

58. Do we know the cause of gravitation?
(See *Astronomy*, note, p. 23.)

283—*1. In what constellation is Job's Coffin? The Letter Y? The Scalene Triangle? The Dipper? The Kids? The Triangles?*

Job's Coffin is in Delphinus; the Letter Y, in Aquarius; the Scalene Triangle, in Aries; the Big Dipper, in Ursa Major; the Kids, in Auriga; and the Triangles, between Almach and Arietis.

2. Name some facts in the solar system for which the Nebular Hypothesis fails to account.

It is very difficult to explain, on the basis of the Nebular Hypothesis, why the axes of certain of the planets are so greatly inclined, and, especially, why the velocity of the rotation of the inner moon of Mars should so far exceed that of Mars itself.

3. Which is probably hotter, a yellow or a red star?
(See *Astronomy*, note, p. 241.)

When we heat a piece of iron, it first becomes red-hot, then, as the temperature rises, other colors appear, until, finally, it becomes dazzling white. (See *Physics*, p. 183.)

4. Are any of the stars likely to collide with each other?

Nothing strikes the astronomer more forcibly than the thought of the *desolateness of space*. A vast gulf, more than twenty-five trillions of miles in width, separates Neptune from the nearest fixed star. It has been estimated that the average distance between two of the sixty millions of fixed stars visible to our largest telescopes, is about nine millions of millions of miles. With this amount of "elbow-room," a collision between any two such remote neighbors would be almost impossible. Yet, Sir Wm. Thomson remarks: "It is as sure that collisions must occur between great masses moving through space, unless guided in their paths, as it is that ships, steered without intelligence, could not cross and recross the Atlantic for thousands of years with immunity from collisions."

5. Is the real day longer or shorter than the apparent one?
(See *Astronomy*, p. 264.)

6. Do we ever see the stars?
(See *Astronomy*, p. 203.)

7. What fixed star is nearest the earth?
(See *Astronomy*, pp. 204, 241.)

8. How often is Polaris on the meridian of a place?

As Polaris revolves about the true pole in a circle, the radius of which is nearly $1\frac{1}{2}°$, it follows that in every twenty-four hours it is once on the meridian below the pole, and, also, once above it. The diameter of this circle is the length of Orion's Belt, the stars at the right and the left of the central one representing the distance the polar star goes to the right and left of the pole.

9. How do we know that the stars are suns?
(See *Astronomy*, pp. 205, 261.)

Spectrum analysis proves this to be the fact.

10. Can a watch keep apparent time?
(See *Astronomy*, p. 265.)

11. How could a child be eight years old before a return of its birthday?

An infant born on Feb. 29, 1796, did not have a birthday proper until Feb. 29, 1804, since the year 1800, not being divisible by 400, was not a leap-year. Many other such dates may be named.

12. When will a watch and a sun-dial agree?
(See *Astronomy*, p. 265.)

13. What star will be the Pole Star next after Polaris?
(See *Astronomy*, p. 217.)

14. Why is the birthday of Washington celebrated on Feb. 22, when he was born Feb. 11, 1732 (O. S.)?
(See *Astronomy*, note, p. 312.)

15. Does the tide have any effect on the length of the day?
(See *Astronomy*, notes, pp. 89, 303.)

16. Will the Big Dipper always look as it does now?
(See *Astronomy*, note, p. 217.)

The following figure, taken from Proctor's *Easy Star Lessons*, represents the location of the seven stars comprising the Big Dipper, as they will be seen 100,000 years hence:

$$\kappa_* \qquad \varepsilon^* \qquad \delta_* \qquad\qquad\qquad {}^{*\alpha} \\ \qquad\quad *\eta \qquad\qquad *\gamma \qquad\qquad *\beta$$

17. How many times does the earth turn on its axis every year?
(See *Astronomy*, p. 264.)

18. Does the spectroscope tell us any thing concerning the constitution of the moon, or any of the planets?

These bodies shine, in general, by reflected light; therefore, the light examined comes from the sun. By comparing this reflected light with solar light, the change produced by the planet's atmosphere may be detected. The lunar spectrum exactly accords with the solar spectrum. The spectra of Venus, Mars, Jupiter, and Saturn contain absorption lines indicating aqueous vapor. Read Schellen's *Spectrum Analysis*, p. 333.

19. When the United States bought Alaska from Russia, the calendar used there was found to be one day ahead of our reckoning. Why was this?

IN DESCRIPTIVE ASTRONOMY. 123

One going around the world westward will *lose* a day in his reckoning; one going eastward will *gain* a day. The Alaska calendar was established by those who came from the West to this continent, and their Tuesday corresponded to our Monday.

20. *Why do the dates of the solstices and equinoxes vary a day in different years?*

(See *Astronomy*, p. 99)

Leap-year advances the dates one day.

21. *Why are not forenoon and afternoon of the same day, as given in the almanac, of equal length?*

(See *Astronomy*, p. 265.)

Apparent noon marks the middle of the day; but *mean* noon may be either before or after the apparent noon; *i.e.*, the time when the real sun is on the meridian.

22. *In what part of the heavens (in our latitude) do the stars apparently move from west to east?*

The northern circumpolar constellations revolve about the North Pole, and, during a part of their paths, they apparently move from west to east.

23. *What year was only nine months and six days long?*

(See *Astronomy*, note, p. 312.)

24. *What day will be the last day of the nineteenth century?*

December 31, 1900.

25. *If one should watch the sky, on a winter's evening, from 6 P.M. to 6 A.M., what portion of the celestial sphere would he be able to see?*

All that is ever seen in his latitude.

26. *How do we know that the moon has little, if any, atmosphere?*

Because when the moon occults a star, there is no refraction of the star's true place.

27. In Greenland, at what part of the year will the midnight sun be seen due north?

At all places whose latitude is 66° 30′ N., the sun will be on the northern horizon at midnight of the summer solstice. At all places north of the Arctic Circle the sun will remain above the horizon, even at midnight, for a certain portion of the summer, the number of days increasing with the latitude. Read Ball's *Elements of Astronomy*, p. 142.

28. Can you give any other proof of the rotundity of the earth, besides that named in the text (p. 85)?

(See *Astronomy*, note, p. 299.)

A sphere is the only body that always presents to us the form of a circle, no matter in what direction we view it. At sea, the circular form of the horizon is even more evident than on land.

29. Point out the error in the following passage from Byron's "Darkness," where the poet, in describing the effect of the sun's destruction, says:

" I had a dream, ...
    ... which was not all a dream ;
The bright sun was extinguished, and the stars
Did wander darkling in the external space
Rayless and pathless."

The fixed stars would be unaffected by the extinction of the sun's light.

30. Explain the remark of the First Carrier in Scene I., Act II., King Henry IV.: "An't be not four by the day, I'll be hanged: Charles' wain is over the new chimney."

(See *Astronomy*, note, p. 311.)

Since the two great stars which mark the summit and the foot of the Cross have nearly the same right ascension, it follows that the constellation is almost perpendicular at the moment when it passes the meridian. This circumstance is known to every nation that lives beyond the tropics or in the Southern Hemisphere. It has been observed at what hour of the night, in different seasons, the Cross of the south is erect or inclined. It is a time-piece that advances very regularly near four min-

utes a day, and no other group of stars exhibits to the naked eye an observation of time so easily made. How often have we heard our guides exclaim in the savannas of Venezuela, or in the desert extending from Lima to Truxillo, "Midnight is past, the Cross begins to bend!" How often those words reminded us of that affecting scene, where Paul and Virginia, seated near the sources of the river of Lataniers, conversed together for the last time, and where the old man, at the sight of the Southern Cross, warns them that it is time to separate.
—HUMBOLDT.

31. Why does not the earth move with equal velocity in all parts of its orbit?

Because at perihelion it is nearer the sun than when in aphelion, and hence the attraction is stronger.

32. How many Jovian-years old are you?

A Jovian-year equals 11.86 earth-years.

33. Why is the sky blue?

The blue light of the firmament is light reflected by solid particles—generally of aqueous vapor—in the air. It is noticeable that early in the morning and late at night, when the sun's rays fall obliquely upon the atmosphere, they are polarized by reflection. The reflected light is blue; the transmitted light of the sky is orange or red. (Read Tyndall's *Light*, p. 152.)

34. At what season of the year does Christmas occur in Australia?
(See *Astronomy*, Art. vii., p. 98.)

35. What causes the apparent movement of the sun north and south?
(See *Astronomy*, p. 95.)

It is caused by the fact that the axis of the earth is inclined to the plane of the ecliptic, while the earth is revolving about the sun.

36. On what part of the earth is the twilight the longest? The shortest?
(See *Astronomy*, p. 116; *Manual*, p. 116.)

"Where the air is unusually full of condensed vapor, as occurs in polar regions, the twilight is greatly lengthened; where the air is unusually dry, as occurs in the tropics, twilight is said sometimes to be shortened to fifteen minutes."

37. Name the causes which make our summer longer than winter.
(See *Astronomy*, p. 102.)

38. Why is not total darkness produced when a dense cloud passes between us and the sun?
(See *Astronomy*, p. 117.)

39. Why does the time of the tide vary each day?
(See *Astronomy*, p. 148.)

40. Why is an annular longer than a total eclipse?
(See *Astronomy*, p. 140.)

41. Why is it colder in winter than in summer?
(See *Astronomy*, pp. 97, 98.)

42. Do the solar spots affect our weather?
(See *Astronomy*, p. 48.)

43. Can the moon be eclipsed in the day-time?
(See *Astronomy*, p. 114.)

44. Why are the sidereal days of uniform length?

Because of the almost absolute uniformity of the earth's rotation.

45. Why are not the solar days of uniform length?
(See *Astronomy*, p. 266.)

46. What do the moon's phases prove?

The moon's phases prove that she is spherical, and shines by the reflected light of the sun.

47. Why do the sun and moon appear flattened when near the horizon?
(See *Astronomy*, p. 115.)

48. How many stars can we see with the naked eye?

No one sees more than 6,000, and few more than 4,000 stars.

49. *Is there ever an annular eclipse of the moon?*
(See *Astronomy*, p. 146.)

50. *" While the sun rises and sets 365 times, a star rises and sets 366 times." Explain.*
(See *Astronomy*, p. 264.)

51. *How many moons are there in the solar system?*
Twenty have been discovered.

52. *What causes the twinkling of the stars?*
(See *Astronomy*, p. 207.)
Some attribute the twinkling of the stars to the inequality of refraction due to the constant changes in the density of the air, produced by the constant changes in the heat.

53. *Name some of the uses of the stars.*
(See *Astronomy*, pp. 212, 285.)

54. *Describe the methods by which we determine the distance of the sun from the earth.*
(See *Astronomy*, p. 275.)

55. *Why do not the signs and the constellations of the Zodiac agree?*
(See *Astronomy*, pp. 106, 211.)

56. *When we look at the North Star, how long since the light that enters our eye has left that body?*
(See *Astronomy*, p. 218.)

57. *In what direction does a comet's tail generally point?*
(See *Astronomy*, note, p. 306.)

58. *What is the cause of shooting stars?*
(See *Astronomy*, p 182.)

59. *Why does the crescent moon appear larger than the dark body of the moon?*
(See *Astronomy*, p. 123.)

60. *What is the real path of the moon?*
(See *Astronomy*, pp. 123, 301.)

61. *What would be the result if the axis of the earth were parallel to the plane of its orbit?*
(See *Astronomy*, Article xx., p. 103.)

62. Do we see the same stars at different seasons of the year?

(See *Astronomy*, pp. 92, 93.)

63. Why do we not perceive the earth's motion in space?

Because all the objects around us partake of its motion.

64. Did the earth ever shine as a star? Does it now shine as a planet?

The earth, doubtless, shone as a star while it was yet a glowing mass; now, it reflects the sun's light, like the other planets.

65. What is the nebular hypothesis?

(See *Astronomy*, p. 255.)

66. What is the cause of the solar spots?

(See *Astronomy*, p. 54.)

67. Would it make the new moon "drier" or "wetter" if the moon's path ran north of, instead of on, the ecliptic at the time of new moon?

The moon's latitude varies from 5° N. to 5° S. (exactly 5° 8' 47" 9). If the new moon were 5° N., this would increase the angle of $72\tfrac{1}{2}°$ (note, p. 30) to $77\tfrac{1}{2}°$, and thus make the line joining the moon's cusps more nearly parallel to the horizon. It may be easily seen that whenever the plane of the lunar orbit lies so as to carry the moon past conjunction *above* the sun, then the crescent is more nearly horizontal; when *below*, then it is more nearly vertical.

68. Under what conditions are we accustomed to transfer motion?

(See *Astronomy*, pp. 85, 86.)

69. Why do not the planets twinkle?

(See *Astronomy*, note, p. 207.)

70. Why is the horizon a circle?

(See *Manual*, p. 124, Question 28.)

71. What causes are gradually increasing the length of the day?

(See *Astronomy*, notes, pp. 89, 303.)

72. What distance does the moon gain in her orbit each year?

(See *Astronomy*, notes, pp. 89, 302.)

73. State the general argument which renders it probable that other worlds are inhabited.

(See *Astronomy*, p. 63; also, note, p. 297.)

74. Illustrate the uniformity of Nature. What thought does this suggest?

(See *Astronomy*, p. 55; also, note, p. 207.)

So far as we can judge, the laws of Nature, the properties of matter, etc., are uniform throughout the universe, and reveal the workmanship of one Creator.

75. At what rate are we traveling through space? How is this determined?

The mean orbital velocity of the earth is 18.4 miles per second. Knowing the circumference of its yearly path, the rate of motion is easily calculated.

76. Why does the length of a degree of latitude increase in going from the equator toward either pole of the earth?

Because the form of the earth is not perfectly spherical, but is flattened at the poles and bulged at the equator.

LENGTH OF DEGREE OF LATITUDE.

COUNTRY.	LATITUDE.	LENGTH OF DEGREE.
		Feet.
Sweden	66° 20′ 10″ N.	365744
Sweden	66 19 37	367086
Russia	58 17 37	365368
Russia	56 3 55·5	365291
Prussia	54 58 26	365420
Denmark	54 8 13·7	365087
Hanover	52 32 16·6	365300
England	52 35 45	364971
England	52 2 19·4	364951
France	46 52 2	364872
France	44 51 2·5	364572
Rome	42 59 0	364262
America	39 12 0	363786
India	16 8 21·5	363044
India	12 32 20·8	362956
Peru	1 31 0·4 S.	363626
Cape of Good Hope	33 18 30	364713
Cape of Good Hope	35 43 20	364060

77. How can you detect the yearly motion of the sun among the stars?

(See *Astronomy*, first note, p. 94.)

78. Have you actually traced the movement of any one of the planets, so as to understand its peculiar and irregular wandering among the stars?

Pupils should be encouraged to watch the various movements of the heavenly bodies.—Read a thoughtful and suggestive article upon Astronomy in High Schools, in *Popular Science Monthly*, Vol. xx., p. 300.

79. How do you explain the varied aspect of the heavens in the different seasons of the year?

(See *Astronomy*, p. 92.)

80. How does the spinning of a top illustrate the subject of precession?

(See *Astronomy*, p. 109.)

81. Why do solar eclipses come on from the west and cross to the east, while lunar eclipses come on from the east and cross to the west?

The moon is moving from west to east around the earth. In a solar eclipse, her shadow first strikes the western edge of the sun; in a lunar eclipse, the eastern edge of the moon first strikes the shadow of the earth.

The *monthly* motion of the moon from west to east should be carefully distinguished from the *daily* motion caused by the earth's rotation.

82. Newcomb, in his Astronomy, says that, "If, when the moon is near the meridian, an observer could in a moment jump from New York to Liverpool, keeping his eye fixed upon that body, he could see her apparently jump in the opposite direction about the same distance." Explain.

This is an illustration of transferred motion.

83. When, and by whom, was the basis of the calendar we now use fully established?

The Roman calendar had become involved in confusion,

when Julius Cæsar, who possessed no little astronomical knowledge, called to his assistance a Greek astronomer named Sosigenes, and adjusted the civil year to the astronomical year. By intercalating the extra day of leap year, he introduced what is known as the Julian Calendar, which is still in use.

The Persian Calendar, invented in the eleventh century as a correction of the Julian, is remarkable for its accuracy; it consists in making every fourth year bissextile seven times in succession, and making the change for the eighth time in the fifth year instead of the fourth. This is equivalent to reckoning the tropical year as $365\frac{8}{33}$ days, which exceeds the period determined by astronomers only by 0.0001823 of a day, or only $\frac{2}{3}$ of a second, so that it would require a great number of centuries to displace sensibly the commencement of the civil year.

The Gregorian Calendar usually employed is somewhat less exact, but it is more easily reduced to days, years, and centuries, which is one of the most important objects of a calendar. It consists in employing a bissextile year every fourth year, suppressing three bissextiles in three centuries, and replacing one in the fourth. Thus in every 400 years there are reckoned only 97 leap years, making the length of the year $365\frac{97}{400}$, which exceeds the tropical year by 0.0002581 of a day, or very nearly one second.

If, following the analogy of the Gregorian Calendar, our successors shall suppress a bissextile every 4,000 years, so as to make 969 instead of 970 leap years in that interval, the length of the year would become $365\frac{969}{4000}$ days, or 365.2422500 days, instead of 365.242219 days, as determined by observation.— Haughton's *Astronomy*.

84. *How much is the Russian reckoning of time behind ours?*

The Russian reckoning is twelve days behind us.

85. *Is there any gain in having the astronomical and the calendar year agree?*

It is difficult to show what practical object is attained by such coincidence. It is important that summer and winter, seed-time and harvest, shall occur at the same time of the year through several successive generations; but it is not of the slightest importance that they should occur now at the same time that they did 5,000 years ago.—Read Newcomb's *Astronomy*, p. 50.

86. *What religious festival is fixed each year by the motion of the moon?*

Easter occurs on the Sunday after the first full moon following the spring equinox.—Read article on Easter, in Appletons' *Cyclopedia*.

87. *Why can we, at different times, see both poles of the planet Mars?*

Because the axis of the planet is so much inclined to the plane of the ecliptic.

88. *What famous astronomical discovery was made on the first day of this century?*

(See *Astronomy*, p. 155.)

89. *Do the stars rise and set at the poles?*

(See *Astronomy*, p. 102.)

"At one of the poles of the earth, the axis of the earth's rotation would be vertical, and pass through the zenith, and consequently all the celestial objects would appear to travel in horizontal circles, parallel to the horizon, traversing these horizontal circles once in 23 hours 56 minutes 4 seconds."

90. *Name and locate the stars of the first magnitude which are seen in our sky.*

The twenty brightest stars in the heavens, or first magnitude stars, are as follows: they are given in the order of brightness.—LOCKYER.

Sirius,	in the constellation	Canis Major.
Canopus,	"	Argo.
Alpha,	"	Centaur.
Arcturus,	"	Boötes.
Rigel,	"	Orion.
Capella,	"	Auriga.

Vega,	in the constellation	Lyra.
Procyon,	"	Canis Minor.
Betelgeuse,	"	Orion.
Achernar,	"	Eridanus.
Aldebaran,	"	Taurus.
Beta Centauri,	"	Centaur.
Alpha Crucis,	"	Crux.
Antares,	"	Scorpio.
Altair,	"	Aquila.
Spica,	"	Virgo.
Fomalhaut,	"	Piscis Australis.
Beta Crucis,	"	Crux.
Pollux,	"	Gemini.
Regulus,	"	Leo.

91. Name three bright stars which lie near the first meridian.

a Andromedæ; γ Pegasi; and β Cassiopeiæ.

92. What events were transpiring in our history a Saturnian century ago?

A Saturnian-year equals 29.45 Earth-years; a "Saturnian century ago" was, therefore, 2,945 years since, or about 1060 B.C. This was about the time of the rise of Tyre, the reign of King David, etc.—Read Barnes' *General History*, p. 79.

93. What is the sun's declination at the winter solstice? At the autumnal equinox?

(1.) $23\frac{1}{2}°$ S. (2.) 0.

94. Will the width of the terrestrial zones always remain exactly as now?

(See *Astronomy*, p. 111.)

95. Is it always noon at 12 o'clock?

(See *Manual*, p. 123, Question 21.)

96. When the sun's declination is $23\frac{1}{2}°$ N., in what sign is he then located, and what is his R. A.?

(See *Astronomy*, p. 31.)

This is the time of the summer solstice, and the sun is in Cancer, the fourth sign.

97. What is the apparent diameter of the sun?

The mean apparent diameter of the sun is 32′.

98. How can a sailor find his latitude and longitude at sea?

(See *Astronomy*, p. 280.)

99. How many miles on the solar disk represent a second of apparent diameter?

1″ on the solar disk equals 450.3 miles.—YOUNG. "The spider-line used in a large telescope will cover a portion of the sun's surface ¼ of a second in breadth, or hide a strip over 100 miles wide."

100. At what latitude will there be twilight during the entire midsummer night?

(See *Manual*, p. 114, Question 23.)

When the sun crosses the meridian at midnight, its distance below the horizon is greater than when the sun is at any other part of its diurnal path. If, therefore, the depression of the sun below the horizon at midnight be not greater than 18°, the sun will, during the entire night, be within 18° of the horizon, and hence the twilight will be continuous.—It will be noticed in solving all the problems connected with twilight (as, for example, Question 23, p. 114, and Question 27, p. 124), that the result will be slightly changed if the exact amount of the obliquity of the ecliptic (23° 27′ 15″) be used, instead of the ordinary statement, 23½°.

ADDED QUESTIONS AND ANSWERS.

1. Did Tycho Brahe have a telescope?

No. Galileo invented the telescope.

2. Suppose one should watch the sky, on a winter's evening, from 6 P.M. to 6 A.M., what portion of the celestial sphere would he see?

All that is ever seen in his latitude.

3. How do we find what proportion of the sun's heat reaches the earth?

Calculate the surface of a sphere whose radius is the distance of the earth from the sun, and then estimate what proportion of that area the earth occupies.

4. How do we know the heat of the sun's rays at any planet?

The intensity of the heat and light varies inversely as the square of the distance.

5. Can you give any other proof than that named in the book of the rotundity of the earth?

Aeronauts, when at a proper height, can distinctly see the curving form of the earth's surface.

6. In what way is the force which acts on a spinning-top opposite to that which produces precession?

Gravity, acting on the top, tends to draw C P (Fig. 40) *from* the perpendicular. The attraction of the sun, acting on the bulging mass of the earth's equator, tends to draw C P *toward* the perpendicular.

7. Why is the Tropic of Cancer so called?

When named, the sun was probably in that constellation at the time of the summer solstice. Now, owing to the precession of the equinoxes, the sun is in the constellation Gemini, and to be exact, it should be called the Tropic of Gemini. It is still, however, the sign Cancer, as before. The same reasoning applies to the Tropic of Capricorn, which is now in the constellation Sagittarius.

8. In Greenland, at what part of the year will the midnight sun be seen due north?

At the summer solstice.

9. When is the moon seen high in the eastern sky in the afternoon, long before the sun sets?

During the second quarter before it comes into opposition.

10. Why is the Ecliptic so called?

Because eclipses always occur in or near it.

EXPLAINING MIRRORS AND LENSES.

The author has met with the best success in explaining mirrors and lenses to his pupils by using the following method:

A Concave Mirror.—Holding up before his eye the forefinger of each hand, he represents to the pupil how the rays of light enter his eye *converging;* how he then sees the object on *diverging* rays: thus the visual angle being *increased*, the apparent size of the object is correspondingly increased. By crossing his two forefingers before his eye he represents the focus, and shows how *diverging* rays then enter the eye; the object is seen on *converging* rays, the visual angle is *decreased*, and the apparent size of the object correspondingly decreased.

A Convex Mirror.—Using the fingers in the same way, he illustrates how *diverging* rays enter the eye, the object is seen on *converging* rays, the visual angle is *diminished*, and the apparent size of the object correspondingly diminished. The rays of light are not brought to a focus, hence the second effect of a concave mirror can not be seen.

The same illustration can be used in explaining lenses, remembering that the effect of a convex lens is like that of a concave mirror, and of a concave lens that of a convex mirror.

At the close of the explanation and illustration with the fingers, the following formula is put on the blackboard, and the pupil applies it to each class of mirrors and lenses:

CONVERGING (diverging) RAYS ENTER THE EYE, THE OBJECT IS SEEN ON DIVERGING (converging) RAYS; HENCE THE VISUAL ANGLE IS INCREASED (decreased), AND THE IMAGE IS LARGER (smaller) THAN LIFE.

ASTRONOMY WITH AN OPERA-GLASS.

In schools where there is no telescope, teachers may find valuable suggestions for class observations in the articles entitled "Astronomy with an Opera-Glass," by Garrett P. Serviss, in the *Popular Science Monthly*, April, June, August, and November, 1887, and February, 1888.

TABLE OF THE MINOR PLANETS.*

including all that have been discovered to date (Oct., 1887).

NO.	NAME.	DATE OF DISCOVERY.	DISCOVERER.
1	Ceres	1801, January 1	Piazzi.
2	Pallas	1802, March 28	Olbers.
3	Juno	1804, Sept. 1	Harding.
4	Vesta	1807, March 29	Olbers.
5	Astræa	1845, Dec. 8	Hencke.
6	Hebe	1847, July 1	Hencke.
7	Iris	1847, August 13	Hind.
8	Flora	1847, October 18	Hind.
9	Metis	1848, April 25	Graham.
10	Hygieia	1849, April 12	Gasparis.
11	Parthenope	1850, May 11	Luther.
12	Victoria	1850, Sept. 13	Hind.
13	Egeria	1850, Nov. 2	Gasparis.
14	Irene	1851, May 19	Hind.
15	Eunomia	1851, July 29	Gasparis.
16	Psyche	1852, March 17	Gasparis.
17	Thetis	1852, April 17	Luther.
18	Melpomene	1852, June 24	Hind.
19	Fortuna	1852, August 22	Hind.
20	Massalia	1852, Sept. 19	Gasparis.
21	Lutetia	1852, Nov. 15	Goldschmidt.
22	Calliope	1852, Nov. 16	Hind.
23	Thalia	1852, Dec. 15	Hind.
24	Themis	1853, April 5	Gasparis.
25	Phocæa	1853, April 7	Chacornac.
26	Proserpina	1853, May 5	Luther.
27	Euterpe	1853, Nov. 8	Hind.
28	Bellona	1854, March 1	Luther.
29	Amphitrite	1854, March 1	Marth.
30	Urania	1854, July 22	Hind.
31	Euphrosyne	1854, Sept. 1	Ferguson.
32	Pomona	1854, October 26	Goldschmidt.
33	Polyhymnia	1854, October 28	Chacornac.
34	Circe	1855, April 6	Chacornac.
35	Leucothea	1855, April 19	Luther.
36	Atalanta	1855, October 5	Goldschmidt.
37	Fides	1855, October 5	Luther.
38	Leda	1856, January 12	Chacornac.
39	Lætitia	1856, February 8	Chacornac.

* The numerical order is that adopted by the authority of the Berlin Ephemeria.

TABLE OF THE MINOR PLANETS.

NO.	NAME.	DATE OF DISCOVERY.			DISCOVERER.
40	Harmonia...............	1856,	March	31	Goldschmidt.
41	Daphne.................	1856,	May	22	Goldschmidt.
42	Isis	1856,	May	23	Pogson.
43	Ariadne................	1857,	April	15	Pogson.
44	Nysa....................	1857,	May	27	Goldschmidt.
45	Eugenia...............	1857,	June	27	Goldschmidt.
46	Hestia..................	1857,	August	16	Pogson.
47	Aglaia...................	1857,	Sept.	15	Luther.
48	Doris...................	1857,	Sept.	19	Goldschmidt.
49	Pales	1857,	Sept.	19	Goldschmidt.
50	Virginia................	1857,	October	4	Ferguson.
51	Nemausa..............	1858,	January	22	Laurent.
52	Europa.................	1858,	February	4	Goldschmidt.
53	Calypso................	1858,	April	4	Luther.
54	Alexandra.............	1858,	Sept.	10	Goldschmidt.
55	Pandora...............	1858,	Sept.	10	Searle.
56	Melete*................	1857,	Sept.	9	Goldschmidt.
57	Mnemosyne...........	1859,	Sept.	22	Luther.
58	Concordia.............	1860,	March	24	Luther.
59	Elpis.....................	1860,	Sept.	12	Chacornac.
60	Echo.....................	1860,	Sept.	15	Ferguson.
61	Danaë..................	1860,	Sept.	9	Goldschmidt.
62	Erato	1860,	Sept.	14	Förster & Lesser.
63	Ausonia................	1861,	Feb.	10	Gasparis.
64	Angelina...............	1861,	March	4	Tempel.
65	Cybele..................	1861,	March	8	Tempel.
66	Maia	1861,	April	9	Tuttle.
67	Asia......................	1861,	April	17	Pogson.
68	Leto.....................	1861,	April	29	Luther.
69	Hesperia...............	1861,	April	29	Schiaparelli.
70	Panopea...............	1861,	May	5	Goldschmidt.
71	Niobe...................	1861,	August	13	Luther.
72	Feronia.................	1861,	May	29	Peters & Safford.
73	Clytie...................	1862,	April	7	Tuttle.
74	Galatea................	1862,	August	29	Tempel.
75	Eurydice	1862,	Sept.	22	Peters.
76	Freia....................	1862,	October	21	d'Arrest.
77	Frigga..................	1862,	Nov.	12	Peters.
78	Diana...................	1863,	March	15	Luther.
79	Eurynome.............	1863,	Sept.	14	Watson.
80	Sappho	1864,	May	2	Pogson.
81	Terpsichore...........	1864,	Sept.	30	Tempel.
82	Alcmene...............	1864,	Nov.	27	Luther.

* Goldschmidt at first believed it to be *Daphne* (41), but Schubert finding its period different, called it *Pseudo-Daphne*. It was not seen from 1857 to 1861, when *Luther* rediscovered it, and named it *Melete*.

TABLE OF THE MINOR PLANETS. 139

NO.	NAME.	DATE OF DISCOVERY.			DISCOVERER.
83	Beatrix...............	1865,	April	26	Gasparis.
84	Clio....................	1865,	August	26	Luther.
85	Io.......................	1865,	Sept.	19	Peters.
86	Semele	1866,	January	4	Tietjen.
87	Sylvia.................	1866,	May	16	Pogson.
88	Thisbe................	1866,	June	15	Peters.
89	Julia...................	1866,	August	6	Stephan.
90	Antiope...............	1866,	October	11	Luther.
91	Ægina.................	1866,	Nov.	4	Stephan.
92	Undina...............	1867,	July	7	Peters.
93	Minerva..............	1867,	August	24	Watson.
94	Aurora	1867,	Sept.	6	Watson.
95	Arethusa.............	1867,	Nov.	23	Luther.
96	Ægle...................	1868,	February	17	Coggia.
97	Clotho	1868,	February	17	Tempel.
98	Ianthe.................	1868,	April	18	Peters.
99	Dike....................	1868,	May	28	Borelly.
100	Hecate................	1868,	July	11	Watson.
101	Helena................	1868,	August	15	Watson.
102	Miriam	1868,	August	22	Peters.
103	Hera....................	1868,	Sept.	7	Watson.
104	Clymene..............	1868,	Sept.	13	Watson.
105	Artemis...............	1868,	Sept.	16	Watson.
106	Dione..................	1868,	October	10	Watson.
107	Camilla...............	1868,	Nov.	17	Pogson.
108	Hecuba...............	1869,	April	2	Luther.
109	Felicitas..............	1869,	October	9	Peters.
110	Lydia..................	1870,	April	19	Borelly.
111	Ate.....................	1870,	August	14	Peters.
112	Iphigenia.............	1870,	Sept.	19	Peters.
113	Amalthea............	1871,	March	12	Luther.
114	Cassandra...........	1871,	July	23	Peters.
115	Thyra..................	1871,	August	6	Watson.
116	Sirona.................	1871,	Sept.	8	Peters.
117	Lomia.................	1871,	Sept.	12	Borelly.
118	Peitho	1872,	March	15	Luther.
119	Althæa................	1872,	April	3	Watson.
120	Lachesis..............	1872,	April	10	Borelly.
121	Hermione	1872,	May	12	Watson.
122	Gerda..................	1872,	July	31	Peters.
123	Brunhilda............	1872,	July	31	Peters.
124	Alceste................	1872,	August	23	Peters.
125	Liberatrix............	1872,	Sept.	11	Prosper Henry.
126	Velleda................	1872,	Nov.	5	Paul Henry.
127	Johanna..............	1872,	Nov.	5	Prosper Henry.
128	Nemesis...............	1872,	Nov.	25	Watson.
129	Antigone.............	1873,	February	5	Peters.
130	Electra,...............	1873,	February	17	Peters.

NO.	NAME.	DATE OF DISCOVERY.			DISCOVERER.
131	Vala...............	1873,	May	26	Peters.
132	Æthra.............	1873,	June	13	Watson.
133	Cyrene	1873,	August	16	Watson.
134	Sophrosyne......	1873,	Sept.	27	Luther.
135	Hertha............	1874,	Feb.	18	Peters.
136	Austria............	1874,	March	18	Palisa.
137	Melibœa..........	1874,	April	21	Palisa.
138	Tolosa.............	1874,	May	19	Perrotin.
139	Juewa.............	1874,	October	10	Watson.
140	Siwa...............	1874,	October	13	Palisa.
141	Lumen	1875,	January	13	Paul Henry.
142	Polana............	1875,	January	28	Palisa.
143	Adria..............	1875,	Feb.	23	Palisa.
144	Vibilia	1875,	June	3	Peters.
145	Adeona...........	1875,	June	3	Peters.
146	Lucina............	1875,	June	8	Borelly.
147	Protogeneia.....	1875,	July	11	Schulhof.
148	Gallia	1875,	August	7	Prosper Henry.
149	Medusa...........	1875,	Sept.	21	Perrotin.
150	Nuwa..............	1875,	October	18	Watson.
151	Abundantia	1875,	Nov.	1	Palisa.
152	Atala..............	1875,	Nov.	2	Paul Henry.
153	Hilda..............	1875,	Nov.	2	Palisa.
154	Bertha............	1875,	Nov.	4	Prosper Henry.
155	Scylla.............	1875,	Nov.	8	Palisa.
156	Xantippe.........	1875,	Nov.	22	Palisa.
157	Dejanira..........	1875,	Dec.	1	Borelly.
158	Koronis...........	1876,	January	4	Knorre.
159	Æmilia............	1876,	January	26	Paul Henry.
160	Una	1876,	February	20	Peters.
161	Athor	1876,	April	18	Watson.
162	Laurentia........	1876,	April	21	Prosper Henry.
163	Erigone	1876,	April	26	Perrotin.
164	Eva.................	1876,	July	12	Paul Henry.
165	Loreley...........	1876,	August	9	Peters.
166	Rhodope	1876,	August	15	Peters.
167	Urda	1876,	August	28	Peters.
168	Sibylla	1876,	Sept.	28	Watson.
169	Zelia...............	1876,	Sept.	28	Prosper Henry.
170	Maria..............	1877,	January	10	Perrotin.
171	Ophelia...........	1877,	January	13	Borelly.
172	Bancis.............	1877,	February	5	Borelly.
173	Ino..................	1877,	August	2	Borelly.
174	Phædra	1877,	Sept.	3	Watson.
175	Andromache....	1877,	October	1	Watson.
176	Idunna............	1877,	October	14	Peters.
177	Irma...............	1877,	Nov.	5	Prosper Henry.
178	Belisana	1877,	Nov.	6	Palisa.
179	Clytemnestra...	1877,	Nov.	12	Watson.

TABLE OF THE MINOR PLANETS.

NO.	NAME.	DATE OF DISCOVERY.	DISCOVERER.
180	Garumna...............	1878, January 29	Perrotin.
181	Eucharis...............	1878, February 2	Cottenot.
182	Elsa	1878, February 7	Palisa.
183	Istria...................	1878, February 8	Palisa.
184	Deiopeia...............	1878, February 28	Palisa.
185	Euniko	1878, March 1	Peters.
186	Celuta..................	1878, April 6	Prosper Henry.
187	Lamberta.........	1878, April 11	Coggia.
188	Menippe................	1878, June 18	Peters.
189	Phthia	1878, Sept. 9	Peters.
190	Ismene.................	1878, Sept. 22	Peters.
191	Kolga...................	1878, Sept. 30	Peters.
192	Nausicaa...............	1879, February 17	Palisa.
193	Ambrosia...............	1879, February 28	Coggia.
194	Procne	1879, March 21	Peters.
195	Eurycleia.....	1879, April 22	Palisa.
196	Philomela..............	1879, May 17	Peters.
197	Arete.......	1879, May 21	Palisa.
198	Ampella................	1879, June 13	Borelly.
199	Byblis...................	1879, July 9	Peters.
200	Dynamene.............	1879, July 27	Peters.
201	Penelope...............	1879, August 7	Palisa.
202	Chryseis................	1879, Sept. 11	Peters.
203	Pompeia................	1879, Sept. 25	Peters.
204	Callisto......	1879, October 8	Palisa.
205	Martha.................	1879, October 13	Palisa.
206	Hersilia................	1879, October 13	Peters.
207	Hedda..................	1879, October 17	Palisa.
208	Lacrymosa............	1879, October 21	Palisa.
209	Dido.....................	1879, October 22	Peters.
210	Isabella	1879, Nov. 12	Palisa.
211	Isolda...................	1879, Dec. 10	Palisa.
212	Medea..................	1880, February 6	Palisa.
213	Liliæa...................	1880, February 16	Peters.
214	Aschera................	1880, March 1	Palisa.
215	Œnone	1880, April 7	Knorre.
216	Cleopatra.......... ...	1880, April 10	Palisa.
217	Eudora.................	1880, August 30	Coggia.
218	Bianca	1880, Sept. 4	Palisa.
219	Thusnelda	1880, Sept. 30	Palisa.
220	Stephania.............	1881, May 20	Palisa.
221	Eos	1882, January 18	Palisa.
222	Lucia....	1882, February 9	Palisa.
223	Rosa....................	1882, March 9	Palisa.
224	Oceana	1882, March 30	Palisa.
225	Henrietta......	1882, April 19	Palisa.
226	Weringia...............	1882, July 10	Palisa.
227	Philosophia...........	1882, August 12	Paul Henry.
228	Agathe.	1882, August 10	Palisa.

TABLE OF THE MINOR PLANETS.

NO.	NAME.	DATE OF DISCOVERY.	DISCOVERER.
229	Adelinda	1882, August 22	Palisa.
230	Athamantis	1882, Sept. 3	De Ball.
231	Vindobona	1882, Sept. 10	Palisa.
232	Russia	1883, January 31	Palisa.
233	Asterope	1883, May 11	Borelly.
234	Barbara	1883, August 13	Peters.
235	Caroline	1883, Nov. 29	Palisa.
236	Honoria	1884, April 26	Palisa.
237	Cœlestina	1884, June 27	Palisa.
238	Hypatia	1884, July 1	Knorre.
239	Adrastea	1884, August 18	Palisa.
240	Vanadis	1884, August 27	Borelly.
241	Germania	1884, Sept. 12	Luther.
242	Kriemhild	1884, Sept. 22	Palisa.
243	Ida	1884, Sept. 29	Palisa.
244	Sita	1884, October 14	Palisa.
245	Vera	1885, February 6	Pogson.
246	Asporina	1885, March 6	Borelly.
247	Eukrate	1885, March 14	Luther.
248	Lameia	1885, June 5	Palisa.
249	Ilse	1885, August 17	Peters.
250	Bettina	1885, Sept. 3	Palisa.
251	Sophia	1885, October 4	Palisa.
252	Clementina	1885, October 27	Perrotin.
253	Mathilda	1885, Nov. 12	Palisa.
254	Augusta	1886, March 31	Palisa.
255	Oppavia	1886, March 31	Palisa.
256	Walpurga	1886, April 3	Palisa.
257	Silesia	1886, April 5	Palisa.
258	Tyche	1886, May 4	Luther.
259	Altheia	1886, June 28	Peters.
260	Huberta	1886, October 3	Palisa.
261	Prymno	1886, October 31	Peters.
262	Valda	1886, Nov. 3	Palisa.
263	Dresda	1886, Nov. 3	Palisa.
264	Libussa	1886, Dec. 17	Peters.
265	Anna	1887, February 25	Palisa.
266	Aline	1887, May 17	Palisa.
267	Tirza	1887, May 27	Charlois.
268		1887, June 9	Borelly.
269		1887, Sept. 21	Palisa.
270		1887, October 8	Peters.
271		1887, October 16	Knorre.

From this Table, it will be observed that, next to Palisa, of Vienna, Austria, the one investigator who has discovered the largest number of asteroids is our own Dr. Peters, of Clinton, N. Y. It is probable that all the larger asteroids have now been identified.

ANSWERS

TO THE

PRACTICAL QUESTIONS

IN THE

HYGIENIC PHYSIOLOGY.

23—1. *Why does not a fall hurt a child as much as it does a grown person?*

The bones of a child are largely cartilaginous, and so do not transmit a shock, or readily yield to a blow. They are also well padded with fat.

2. *Should a young child ever be urged to stand or walk?*

No; bow-legs are often caused by the premature use of the lower limbs in standing or walking. Nature is the best guide in such matters.

3. *What is meant by "breaking one's neck"?*

The dislocation of the vertebræ and consequent injury of the spinal cord.

4. *Should chairs or benches have straight backs?*

The backs should conform to the natural shape of the spine. This tends to prevent curvatures and other distortions of the vertebral column.

5. *Should a child's feet be allowed to dangle from a high seat?*

The position is as unnatural and painful for a child as for a grown person.

6. *Why can we tell whether a fowl is young by pressing on the point of the breast-bone?*

Because that part of the breast-bone is not ossified in a young fowl.

7. *What is the use of the marrow in the bones?*

It contains the blood-vessels carrying material for the growth of the bone, and also diffuses any shock which the bone may receive.

8. *Why is the shoulder so often put out of joint?*

Because of the shallowness of the socket in the scapula.

9. *How can you tie a knot in a bone?*

By removing the mineral matter, and thus softening a rib-bone, a knot can be easily tied in it.

10. *Why are high pillows injurious?*

They elevate the head, and so give an unnatural position to the spine. For the pads between the vertebræ to assume their proper shape during the night they should be relieved of all pressure.

11. *Is a stooping posture a healthy position?*

No. Such a posture, made habitual, contracts the chest, changes the outline of the spine, and diminishes the vitality of the system.

12. *Ought a boot to have a heel-piece?*

A low and broad heel-piece probably aids in walking; a narrow or high one weakens and enlarges the ankle, produces bunions, corns, etc., by throwing the weight forward upon the toes, and makes the gait exceedingly ungraceful.

13. *Why should one always sit and walk erect?*

Because then all the organs are in their natural position. An erect carriage is as conducive to health as to beauty.

14. *Why does a young child creep rather than walk?*
(See *Physiology*, p. 50.)

Its bones not yet being fully ossified, nature teaches it not to bear its weight upon them. Besides, it has not yet learned the difficult art of balancing itself.

15. What is the natural direction of the big toe?

The natural direction of the big toe is in a line with the long axis of the foot, but the conventional boot, which insists upon an even-sided symmetry, and often upon a narrow tip, tends to crowd the extremity of this toe toward the middle line of the sole. If well-developed feet are placed side by side and heel to heel, the two great toes will be found to be parallel to each other, and to touch each other almost to their very ends. If the same feet, clad in the shoes of the period, are placed in the same position, it will be found that, while the heels are in contact, the tips of the two great toes will be considerably separated.

16. What is the difference between a sprain and a fracture? A dislocation?

In a sprain, the ligaments which bind the bones of a joint are strained, twisted, or torn from their attachments; in a fracture, the bone itself is broken; in a dislocation, the bone is displaced from its socket.

17. Does the general health of the system affect the strength of the bones?

Certainly. Impoverished blood will not make healthy bone.

46—1. What class of lever is the foot when we lift a weight on the toes?

The third class. The ankle-joint is the fulcrum, the weight is at the toes, and the power is in front of the ankle, where the muscle which lifts the toes (the extensor digitorium) is attached to the foot.

2. Explain the movement of the body backward and forward, when resting upon the thigh-bone as a fulcrum.

The weight is at the center of gravity of the head and trunk, high above the hip-joints, where the fulcrum is situated. The flexor muscles of the thigh are the power, and act close to the fulcrum. The weight is sometimes directly over the fulcrum, and may be on any side of it. This seems to the author to be an example of the first or second class of lever. Huxley gives it as an illustration of the third class.

3. What class of lever do we use when we lift the foot while sitting down?

The third class. The fulcrum is the knee-joint; the weight is at the center of gravity of the foot and leg, and the power is applied by the ligament which passes over the patella.

4. Explain the swing of the arm from the shoulder.
(See *Physiology*, p. 34.)

The third class. The fulcrum is the shoulder-joint; the weight is at the center of gravity of the arm and hand, and the power is applied by the biceps or triceps muscle at its attachment near the elbow.

5. What class of lever is used in bending our fingers?

The fulcrum is at the junction of the finger with the palm; the weight is at the center of gravity of the finger, and may play about the fulcrum as stated in second question. It is the third class of lever, especially when force is exerted at the extremity of the fingers.

6. What class of lever is our foot when we tap the ground with our toes?
(See *Physiology*, Fig. 14, *k*.)

The first class. The weight is at the toe when the force is exerted; the fulcrum is at the ankle; and the power is applied by the gastrocnemius muscle at its attachment to the heel.

7. What class of lever do we use when we raise ourselves from a stooping position?

The third class. See second question. If we are attempting to lift a heavy burden, the bones act on the principle of the toggle-joint. "When one stoops to take a heavy weight upon his back or shoulder, he puts both the knee and the hip-joints into the condition that the toggle-joint is when it is bent; and then, as he straightens up, the weight is raised by an action of the joints precisely similar to that of the toggle-joint in machinery. In the case of the knee, the straightening of the joints is done by the muscles on the front part of the thigh, that draw up the knee-pan with the tendon attached to it. This is using the principle of the toggle-joint in pressing *upward*. It is also sometimes used in pressing *downward*. In crushing any thing with the heel, we give great force to the blow on the principle of the toggle-joint, by flexing the knee and straightening the limb as we bring down the heel upon the thing to be crushed. In pushing any thing before us, we bend the elbow as preparatory to the act, and then thrust the arm out straight, thus exemplifying the toggle-joint. The horse gives great force to his kick in the same way. The great power exerted by beasts of draught and burden is to be referred very much to the principle of the toggle-joint. When a horse is to draw a heavy load, he bends all his limbs, especially the hinder ones, and then as he straightens them, he starts the load. In this case the ground is the fixed block of the mechanism, the body of the horse to which the load is attached is the movable one, and his limbs are so many toggle-joints. By this application of the principle, we see draught horses move very heavy loads."—HOOKER's *Physiology*. "So (admitting fable to be fact), when the farmer, in answer to his petition for assistance, was commanded by Hercules to exert himself to raise his wagon from the pit, he placed his shoulder against the wheel, and drawing his body up into a crouching attitude, whereby all his joints are flexed, and making his feet the fixed points, by a powerful muscular effort, he straightened the toggle-joints of his limbs, and the wheel was raised from its bed of miry clay. His horses at the same moment extending their joints, the heavily laden wagon was carried beyond the reach of further detention."—GRISCOM.

8. *What class of lever is the foot when we walk?*

In the first stage it is clearly the second class. (See *Physiology*, Fig. 18.) The fulcrum is the ground on which the toes rest; the power is applied by the gastrocnemius muscle (see Fig. 14, *k*) to the heel; the resistance is so much of the weight of the body as is borne by the ankle-joint of the foot, which of course lies between the heel and the toes.

9. Why can we raise a heavier weight with our hand when lifting with the elbow than from the shoulder?

Because we bring the fulcrum nearer the power. In the former case it is at the elbow; in the latter, at the shoulder.

10. What class of lever do we employ when we are hopping, the thigh-bone being bent up toward the body and not used?

In this case the fulcrum is at the hip-joint. The power (which may be assumed to be furnished by the *rectus* muscle* of the front of the thigh) acts upon the knee-cap; and the position of the weight is represented by that of the center of gravity of the thigh and leg, which will lie somewhere between the end of the knee and the hip.—HUXLEY.

11. Describe the motions of the bones when we are using a gimlet.

The radius rolls on the ulna at the elbow, while the ulna rolls on the radius at the wrist. The two combined produce a free, rotary motion.

12. Why do we tire when we stand erect?
(See *Physiology*, p. 37.)

Because so large a number of muscles must be in constant action to maintain this position.

13. Why does it rest us to change our work?

We thereby bring into use a new set of muscles.

14. Why and when is dancing a beneficial exercise?

When dancing is performed out-of-doors, or in a well-ventilated room, and at proper hours, it is doubtless a beneficial exercise, since it employs the muscles and pleasantly occupies the mind. Late at night, in a heated room, with thin clothing and exciting surroundings, it is simply a dangerous dissipation, ruinous to the health, alike of body and soul.

---

* This muscle is attached above to the haunch-bone or *ileum*, and below to the knee-cap. The latter bone is connected by a strong ligament with the *tibia*.

15. Why can we exert greater force with the back teeth than with the front ones?

(See *Physiology*, p. 35.)

The lower jaw is a lever of the second class. In the former case the resistance to be overcome, *i.e.*, the weight, is situated much nearer the power.

16. Why do we lean forward when we wish to rise from a chair?

(See *Popular Physics*, p. 57.)

In order to bring the center of gravity over the feet.

17. Why does the projection of the heel-bone make walking easier?

(See Frontispiece, and also Fig. 18 in *Physiology*.)

It brings the power further from the fulcrum or weight.

18. Does a horse travel with less fatigue over a flat than a hilly country?

No. The variety of travel in a hilly country, other things being equal, tends to rest the horse, and enable him to better endure the fatigue of the journey.

19. Can you move your upper jaw?

All the bones of the face, except the lower jaw, are firmly and immovably articulated with one another and with the cranium.—LEIDY.

20. Are people naturally right or left-handed?

Many persons are naturally either right or left-handed; but most can and should learn to use either hand with equal facility.

21. Why can so few persons move their ears by the muscles?

Perhaps because of lack of practice; more probably, however, the muscles (see *Physiology*, p. 53 and Fig. 14) are developed in few persons.

22. Is the blacksmith's right arm healthier than the left?

By no means. Strength is not essential to health. The right arm may be stronger, but the functions of the left may be as active and well-performed.

23. Boys often, though foolishly, thrust a pin into the flesh just above the knee. Why is it not painful?

The muscles of the leg there end in tendons, which are insensible.

24. Will ten minutes' practice in a gymnasium answer for a day's exercise?

Spasmodic or violent exercise is not beneficial. It should be comparatively quiet, gentle, and continuous to produce the best effect. Moreover, the vitalizing influences of the sun and pure air demand that we should exercise out-of-doors.

25. Why would an elastic tendon be unfitted to transmit the motion of a muscle?

Force would be lost by its transmission through an elastic medium.

26. When one is struck violently on the head, why does he instantly fall?

The body is kept erect only by the constant exercise of many muscles. These perform their functions through the unconscious action of the brain and spinal cord. A blow paralyzes the nervous system, the muscles at once cease to act, and the body falls by its weight.

27. What is the cause of the difference between light and dark meat in a fowl?

The amount of blood which circulates through different parts of the body. The organs of a fowl which are used the most become the darkest.

69—1. If a hair be plucked out, will another grow in its place?

Yes. A new hair will always grow out so long as the papilla at the bottom of the follicle remains uninjured.

2. What causes the hair to "stand on end" when we are frightened? (See *Physiology*, p. 53.)

Many of the unstriated muscular fibers from the true skin pass obliquely down from the surface of the dermis to the under side of the slanting hair-follicles. The contraction of these fibers erects the hairs, and by drawing the follicles to the surface and drawing in a little point of the skin, produces that roughness of the integument called "goose-skin," or *Cutis Anserina*. The standing on end of the hair of the head, as the result of extreme fright, may be partly due to the contraction of such fibers, as well as to the action of the occipito-frontalis muscle.—CUTTER.

3. Why is the skin roughened by riding in the cold? (See *Physiology*, p. 53; also Answer to Question 2.)

4. Why is the back of a washer-woman's hand less water-soaked than the palm?

The difference depends upon the relative abundance of the oil-glands in different parts of the body.

5. What would be the length of the perspiratory tubes in a single square inch of the palm, if placed end to end? (See *Physiology*, p. 61.)

The length of the perspiratory tubes differs not only in different persons but in different parts of the same body. Some authorities estimate the average length at $\frac{1}{4}$ of an inch, while others—and, generally, later authorities—give only $\frac{1}{16}$ of an inch. If we assume the former measurement, we have: $2,800 \times \frac{1}{4}$ in. $= \frac{2800}{4}$ in. $= 58$ ft. 4 in. If the latter, we have $2,800 \times \frac{1}{16}$ in. $= \frac{2800}{16}$ in. $= 14$ ft. 7 in.

6. What colored clothing is best adapted to all seasons? (See *Physiology*, p. 67; *Popular Physics*, p. 260.)

Light-colored clothing is cooler in summer and warmer in winter.

7. What is the effect of paint and powder on the skin? (See *Physiology*, p. 62.)

They fill the pores of the skin, and thus prevent the passage of the perspiration. Moreover, they often contain substances which are poisonous, and being carried in by the absorbents cause disease.

8. *Is water-proof clothing healthful for constant wear?*

No. It retains the insensible perspiration by which waste matter is being constantly thrown off from the system.

9. *Why are rubbers cold to the feet?*

They retain the insensible perspiration. The moisture which gathers absorbs the heat of the feet, and readily conducts it from the body.

10. *Why does the heat seem oppressive when the air is moist?*

In the moisture-laden atmosphere, the evaporation of the insensible perspiration from the surface of the body goes on slowly. The heat, which would otherwise pass off through the pores, is retained in the system.

11. *Why is friction of the skin invigorating after a cold bath?*

(See *Physiology*, p. 64, 65.)

The friction produces heat, expands the veins, etc., on the surface, and, calling the blood in that direction, produces a vigorous circulation. In other words, it causes a reaction.*

---

* Strength in the living body is maintained by the full but natural exercise of each organ; and, as we have seen, the actions of these portions of the nervous system is made dependent upon influences conveyed to them by the sensitive nerves distributed over the various parts of the body. And among these the nerves passing to the skin are the chief. The full access of all healthful stimuli to the surface, and its freedom from all that irritates or impedes its functions, are the first external conditions of the normal vigor of this nervous circle. Among these stimuli, fresh air and pure water hold the first place. Sufficient warmth is second. The great and even wonderful advantages of cleanliness are partly referable to the direct influence of a skin healthily active, open to all the natural stimuli, and free from morbid irritation, upon the nerve-centers of which it is the appointed excitant. This influence is altogether distinct from those cleansing functions which the healthy skin performs for the blood; and in any just estimate of its value is far too important to be overlooked.—HINTON.

12. Why does the hair of domestic animals become roughened in winter?
(See Question 2.)

It is a wise provision of Nature, since more air—a non-conductor of heat—is retained by the hair, and thus the rough winter-coat of an animal is warmer than its smooth summer-coat.

13. Why do fowls spread their feathers before they perch for the night?
(See Question 12.)

This is the same wise provision of Nature to protect the fowl against the chilliness of the night. More air is confined by the roughened feathers, and thus the internal heat of the bird is prevented from radiating.

14. How can an extensive burn cause death by congestion of the lungs?
(See *Physiology*, p. 63.)

The insensible perspiration is stopped upon the burned surface, and the excretions are sent to the lungs, which are overworked and overloaded by the excess.

15. Why do we perspire so profusely after drinking cold water?

The vital organs being chilled for an instant, the blood is sent to the surface, a reaction is produced, the skin acts more vigorously as an excretory organ, and the insensible perspiration is thrown off more rapidly.

16. What are the best means of preventing skin diseases, colds, and rheumatism?

The skin should be kept in a healthy state by bathing, rubbing, etc. Exposure to sudden changes of temperature should be avoided as far as possible. Flannel worn next the skin, in all seasons of the year, is an excellent precaution against unavoidable exposure.

17. What causes the difference between the hard hand of a blacksmith and the soft hand of a woman?
(See *Physiology*, p. 50.)

The varying thickness of the cuticle.

18. Why should a painter avoid getting paint on the palm of his hand? (See *Physiology*, p. 62.)

19. Why should we not use the soap or the soiled towel at a hotel?

Because of the danger of contracting disease through the absorbents of the skin. (See *Physiology*, p. 62.) There is a similar danger in using a hair-brush or a comb at a barber shop.

20. Which teeth cut like a pair of scissors?

The "back teeth," as we commonly call them, when moved laterally, cut somewhat in this way. In chewing the food, all the "front teeth" act like scissors, as may be readily seen by noticing their movements.

21. Which teeth cut like a chisel?

The incisors, or four front teeth of each jaw, have knife edges; the canine teeth have wedge-shaped edges; the bicuspids and molars have broader crowns. We can work the jaws so as to make the front teeth either pierce like wedges or cut like scissors.

22. Which should be clothed the warmer, a merchant or a farmer?

The merchant is liable to more sudden and violent changes of temperature, and his body is less likely to be hardened by exposure and habit to resist them.

23. Why should we not crack nuts with our teeth?

The brittle enamel is very liable to crack, and once broken can never be restored.

24. Do the edges of the upper and lower teeth meet? (See Question 21.)

25. When fatigued, should you take a cold bath?

Certainly not. The system is not vigorous enough to produce a reaction, and the effect might be dangerous.

26. Why is the outer surface of a kid glove finer than the inner?

This illustrates the difference in texture between the cutis and cuticle; the dermis and epidermis.

27. Why will a brunette endure the sun's rays better than a blonde?
(See *Physiology*, p 51.)

The skin is perhaps of a coarser texture, and not so sensitive to heat. May it not be also that the black pigment absorbs the heat and radiates it again rather than transmits it directly to the internal organs? It has also been suggested that there is an increased flow of blood in the darker skin, and hence increased perspiration.

28. Does patent-leather form a healthful covering for the feet?

No. The pores of the leather are partly filled, and hence the insensible perspiration is largely restrained.

29. Why are men more frequently bald than women?

This is to some extent the effect of the close, unventilated head-covering commonly worn by men.

30. On what part of the head does baldness commonly occur?

On that part most fully covered by the hat or cap.

31. What does the combination in our teeth of canines and grinders suggest as to the character of our food?

That we are to eat a mixed diet of vegetable and animal food.*

---

* The question of the use of animal or vegetable food may well be remitted to the arbitrament of nature, as expressed in the desires; by which it would be victoriously decided, in all such climates as ours, in favor of the flesh-eater. But the sufficiency of vegetable food, if widely varied, to maintain health and even strength, is not to be questioned, for those who like it. When we hear that the ancient Persians lived a good deal on water-cress, we naturally connect in our minds their physical inferiority

32. Is a staid, formal promenade suitable exercise?

No. There is an intimate relation between the brain and the muscles. The mind should be pleasantly employed to obtain the full effect of any exercise.* The sports of children are often the very perfection of healthful gymnastic exercises.

33. Is there any danger in changing the warm clothing of our daily wear for the thin one of a party?

Very great. The body is not so well protected as usual against a sudden change of temperature, as in going from a heated room to the carriage, and a cold is often the consequence. This may lay the foundation of fatal disease.

34. Should we retain our overcoat, shawl, or furs, when we come into a warm room?

No. The body will become over-heated, the pores be opened, and the skin be rendered susceptible to the change of temperature when we return into the open air.

---

with the poverty of their diet; but finding, on the other hand, that the Romans, in the best period of the Republic, largely sustained themselves on turnips, and that degeneracy came in as turnips went out, we are compelled to reconsider our opinion. In brief, an exclusively vegetable food may be best suited to those by whom it really is preferred. Children in this respect exhibit the greatest difference; some, with manifest advantage, eat meat in large quantity—others can hardly be prevailed on to taste it, and yet retain perfect vigor. Similar differences, in all probability, exist among adults; but a vegetarianism self-imposed against the promptings of desire, would tend, as a vigorous writer says, to make us "not the children, but the abortions of Paradise."—HINTON.

* The mental operations, like all others, are connected with changes in the material of the body. In all our consciousness the chemical tendencies of the substance of the brain come into play, and thus a chain of action is set up which extends throughout the system. The influence of these brain-changes is felt wherever a nerve travels, and modifies, invigorates, or depraves the action of every part. Experience gives ample proof of this fact to every one, as in the sudden loss of appetite a piece of bad news will cause, or in the watering of the mouth excited by the thought of food. And the history of disease abounds in evidence of a similar kind: hair becoming gray in a single night from sorrow, milk poisoning an infant from an attack of passion in the nurse, permanent discoloration of the skin from terror, are among the instances on record.—HINTON.

35. Which should bathe the oftener, students or outdoor laborers?

This depends entirely on circumstances—the amount of exercise, the individual freedom and character of perspiration, the state of the system, etc. Each case must be decided by itself.

36. Is abundant perspiration injurious?

No. It removes impure matter from the system, and hence may be beneficial. It may, however, weaken the body, and frequent hot baths should therefore be taken only on suitable medical advice.

37. How often should the ablution of the entire body be performed?

For the preservation of perfect health there should be daily morning ablution in cold or cool water, using soap sparingly. A warm or tepid bath, with a free application of soap, may advantageously be taken once a week, followed by a dash of cool water. It is well for children and delicate persons to stand in warm water, having the cold water in an extra tub or basin. They can then, with a large sponge, dash the cold water freely over their bodies, and get the full tonic effect of the cold bath without the coldness or discomfort which might otherwise ensue. A cold bath should always be quickly performed, accompanied by vigorous rubbing to insure the reaction. Children especially should be thoroughly rubbed and completely dried. Above all, let the daily wash be a delight, and not a dread, to the little ones. A reluctant bath, with a hasty dismissal, leaving the skin wet, the blood chilled, and the spirits depressed, not only inflicts upon the helpless and unhappy child a needless misery, but will be likely to result in chapped skin and chronic catarrh, if in nothing worse.

38. Why is cold water better than warm for our daily ablution?

(See *Physiology*, p. 64.)

The daily repetition of the cold bath renders the system less sensitive to changes in atmospheric temperature, the reverse being the case with the warm bath. Still, it should be said that not every one is able to endure the cold bath. If the skin remains cold and blue in spite of friction, it shows that the reaction has not taken place, in which case the bath is an injury. Or, if for some time after the bath the bather feels languid and weary, it indicates that the reaction is too much for his nervous system. But, in most cases, if the habit is formed by beginning first with tepid water, decreasing the temperature gradually, morning by morning, until the bather inures himself to the coldest water, the shock and the reaction will be a luxury he will not willingly abandon. In this connection it may be said that, as water is a better conductor of heat than air, water at a temperature of 75° or 80° will seem cold to most persons (the normal temperature of the body being about 98° Fahr.), though an atmosphere of that degree would seem warm. The temperature of the room should always be higher than that of the water.

39. Why should our clothing always fit loosely?
(See *Physiology*, pp. 14, 67, 96.)

Any thing that impedes circulation is injurious. Loose under-clothing is warmer in winter than tight under-clothing, on account of the stratum of air between the body and the garment. (See Question 12.) The effects of tight-lacing are well known.* Too close-fitting sleeves interfere with the venous circulation of the arm, and tend to make the fingers cold and blue; while the pressure upon the nerves, which lie not far

---

* The evil effects of tight-lacing are not all nor always in the future. Signs of distress are often quickly apparent; the nose purples, the upper bowels emit croaking sounds, while the lower become unnaturally protuberant; the womb falls, and the breathing and the circulation of blood are so hindered as often to bring on palpitations of the heart and fainting; especially after a full meal or in a close and sultry atmosphere. The long-continued and tight pressure of corsets also wastes and impairs the natural strength of the muscles of the back; so that without the usual lacing there is a most uncomfortable feeling of weakness. The circulation of the blood in the lower part of the lungs, from the severe compression imposed upon them, becomes in an almost stagnant condition, producing languor and a painful sense of lassitude. Continue this constraint, and the cell-life of the lungs, liver, and stomach becomes permanently impaired, laying a sure foundation for disease in these parts whenever the constitutional strength and vigor begin to fail.—*The Ten Laws of Health*, J. R. BLACK.

below the skin, induce neuralgia and numbness in the fingers. A rigid constriction about the arm-pit will frequently result in a swollen hand. Tight elastics should never be worn upon the lower limbs. Aside from all the discomforts and maladies attendant upon the wearing of tight garments, the natural ease and grace of bodily movement are always more or less obstructed.

40. Why should we take special pains to avoid clothing that is colored by poisonous dye-stuffs?
(See *Physiology*, p. 62.)

Because the particles of the poisonous coloring are liable to be absorbed by the skin, and thus taken into the system. The dangerous agent is usually arsenic, which is employed in dyeing bright reds, magentas, aniline reds, and certain greens. Particular care should be taken in the selection of hose. Unfortunately, the pure white stocking has gone out of style, though hygienically it is greatly preferable to the highly (often poisonously) dyed one that has succeeded to fashionable favor.

41. What general principles should guide us as to the length and frequency of baths in salt or fresh water?
(See *Physiology*, pp. 66, 291.)

Sea or river baths should never be prolonged to the extent of sensible fatigue, and consequent inability of reaction. A daily swim taken before breakfast, and limited to twenty minutes at the outside, is to most people the best of tonics. Persons with pale skins (technically termed anæmic, or bloodless), or those who are suffering from heart disease, should not attempt sea or river bathing, or, indeed, any cold bath, except under medical advice.

42. What is the beneficial effect of exercise upon the functions of the skin?
(See *Physiology*, p. 62; also note, p. 42.)

Increased muscular action calls for an extra supply of blood. The heart responds by more rapid beating, the lungs take in more oxygen, and the bodily heat is heightened. To dispose of this superfluous warmth, the oil and perspiratory glands are stimulated to greater activity, the impurities which naturally escape from the body by this avenue are hastened in their exit, and the skin itself becomes soft and moist.

43. How can we best show our admiration and respect for the human body?

By conscientiously observing all the laws of physical hygiene, as well as moral purity.

44. Why is the scar of a severe wound upon a negro sometimes white?

Because the cells containing the pigment or coloring matter were destroyed by the severity of the wound, and have not been restored.

99—1. What is the philosophy of the "change of voice" in a boy?

Up to the age of fourteen or fifteen, there is little or no difference in point of size between the larynx of a boy and that of a girl; but subsequently the former grows proportionately larger, so that at last, in the adult male, the vibrating parts or vocal cords are necessarily longer than in the female. They are also undoubtedly thicker, perhaps even coarser in structure. From all these circumstances the adult male voice is stronger, louder, and of lower pitch than the weaker and higher vocal range accomplished by the female larynx.

The cause of the difference in quality of the voice, known as its *timbre*, is not well known; but it must undoubtedly be dependent on physical, that is to say, structural peculiarities in some part of the laryngeal apparatus.

The production of the different *notes* within the compass of any one individual depends upon alterations in the length and state of tension of the vocal cords, and on their degree of proximity or separation from one another. The higher notes require the vocal cords to be comparatively shorter, tighter, and more closely approximated together; while the lower notes demand opposite conditions. A high note, furthermore, implies greater rapidity in the movement of the air through the glottis; but the quantity of air passing is larger during the production of a low note.

The volume or *loudness* of the voice depends mainly on the combination of quantity of air with greater force of expulsion. Loudness, with clearness, also demands a peculiar resonance up in the nasal cavities and sinuses. Lastly, the unnatural or *falsetto* voice seems also to be produced by some tensive change effected in the upper part of the pharynx at the back of the nose: hence it is called by singers the *head voice*, in contradistinction to the ordinary, or *chest voice*.—MARSHALL.

2. Why can we see our breath on a frosty morning?

The vapor of the breath is condensed by the cold air.

3. When a law of health and a law of fashion conflict, which should we obey?

It depends, of course, whether we prefer to be fashionable or to be healthy, to obey man or God. With too many people the former is of far greater importance, and in selecting an article of dress, few ask or think about the latter. The consequence is seen in the weakened frame, the prevalence of disease, and the shortened life. God's laws written in our bodies can not be violated with impunity.

4. If we use a "bunk" bed, should we pack away the clothes when we first rise in the morning?

No. They should first be thoroughly aired.

5. Why should a clothes-press be well ventilated?

The clothes naturally contain the products of the insensible perspiration, which passing off, pollute the air of the closet.

6. Should the weight of our clothing hang from the waist or the shoulder?

From the shoulder, so as to avoid the constriction of the compressible organs in the abdomen.

7. Describe the effects of living in an overheated room.

(1) The body becomes more sensitive to change, and the susceptibility to colds is greatly increased; (2) the dry, heated air abstracts the moisture from the skin, rendering it dry, hard, and incapable of performing its normal functions.

8. What habits impair the power of the lungs?

Above all others, those of a leaning posture, tight-lacing, and ill-ventilation.

9. For full, easy breathing in singing, should we use the diaphragm and lower ribs or the upper ribs alone?

Nearly all the inspirations are effected by the movements of the diaphragm and the inferior ribs only. From time to time a deeper and more complete inspiration causes the thorax to rise, not simultaneously, but successively at the base, then at the apex. In the first case the respiration is *diaphragmatic;* when the lower and middle ribs are raised, it is termed *lateral;* and, lastly, when the first rib and clavicle take part in the movement, it is costo-superior or *clavicular.* In diaphragmatic respiration, as M. Mandl has observed, the larynx is immovable, the inspiration is easy, without effort, and permits exertion in singing or in gymnastics for a long time and without fatigue. On the contrary, persons who respire principally by the upper ribs are easily fatigued, and very soon out of breath. This is seen in women when the corset compresses the base of the chest, and in singers who adopt, on erroneous principles, the bad habit of clavicular respiration. In this last method of inspiration the larynx is drawn down by the contraction of the external muscles, and its action becomes painful. The effort of the inspiratory muscles rapidly induces fatigue, and the inspiration, always incomplete, becomes also more frequent. Diaphragmatic respiration is practiced by mountaineers, gymnasts, and skillful singers—a habit induced either by instinct, or a well-directed education.—*Wonders of the Human Body.*

10. Why is it better to breathe through the nose than the mouth?

The air passing through the nostrils becomes filtered of its coarse impurities, and the chill is taken off before it strikes against the tender, mucous surfaces of the larynx.

11. Why should not a speaker talk while returning home on a cold night after a lecture?

The cold air will strike against the vocal apparatus when inflamed and peculiarly sensitive.

12. What part of the body needs the loosest clothing?

The abdomen; because of the delicate organs within, unprotected by a bony covering.

13. What part needs the warmest?

The feet, because they are furthest from the center of heat and motion, and most exposed to cold and wet: and the neck and shoulders, since here are located the delicate organs of voice and respiration.

14. Why is a "spare bed" generally unhealthful?

Because it is apt to be damp and unventilated.

15. Is there any good in sighing?
(See *Physiology*, p. 82.)

It probably brings up the "arrears" of respiration.

16. Should a hat be thoroughly ventilated? How?

1. Certainly, as the heated, foul air is injurious. 2. Several openings should be made on the sides near the band. A single hole at the top is quite insufficient for ventilation.

17. Why do the lungs of people who live in cities become of a gray color?

Probably because of the deposition of carbonaceous particles which penetrate the substance of the tissues. The coloring is permanent, like tattooing, where India-ink is pricked beneath the skin.

18. How would you convince a person that a bedroom should be aired?

Take him from the fresh, pure, invigorating out-door atmosphere into the close, depressing air of the bedroom, when first vacated in the morning, and his sense of smell will satisfy him of the need of ventilation.

19. What persons are most liable to catarrh, consumption, etc.?
(See *Physiology*, p. 85.)

The victims of lung-starvation.

20. If a person is plunged under water, will any enter his lungs?

No. The epiglottis will close involuntarily, and prevent the admission of water.

21. Are bed-curtains healthful?

No. They prevent the free circulation of the air, and confine the waste products thrown off from the body.

22. Why do some persons take "short breaths" after a meal?

The distention of the stomach prevents the free action of the lungs. If such persons are not given to gluttony, the lungs are small or the other organs misplaced.

23. What is the special value of public parks?

They bring fresh air, sunshine, green grass and trees within the reach of all. They are truly the "breathing-holes of a city." They are thus of incalculable benefit both on account of their sanitary and moral influence.

24. Can a person become used to bad air, so that it will not injure him?

The system may come to endure without complaint, but, sooner or later, it never fails to inflict full punishment for the infraction of nature's laws.

25. Why do we gape when we are sleepy?
(See Question 15.)

The stretching of the nerves may perhaps serve to restore the equilibrium of the nervous influence, disturbed by the attention being fixed during the day upon some absorbing occupation.

26. Is a fashionable waist a model of art in sculpture or painting?

The Venus of Milo, in the Louvre at Paris, is the beau-ideal of symmetry and beauty, yet the form indicates not a "wasp-waist," but the full, free, flowing outlines of nature. The sculptor and painter in copying the human figure can make no improvement on its Divine Maker.

27. Should a fire-place be closed?
(See *Physiology*, p. 99.)

No. It is a most efficient means of ventilation.

28. Why does embarrassment or fright cause a stammerer to stutter still more painfully?

Stuttering is mainly a nervous disorder, and hence any excitement tends to increase the impediment of the speech.

29. In the organs of voice, what parts have somewhat the same office as the case of a violin and the sounding-board of a piano?
(See *Popular Physics*, p. 186.)

The pharynx, the mouth, and the nasal passages all act by resonance to modify the voice.

30. Why should we be careful not to "take the breath" of a sick person?

Because, in this manner, special disease germs may be directly transferred from the lungs of the sick person into our own. It is well never to "take the breath" of any person, sick or well, since impurities are constantly passing off from every human system through the avenue of the lungs.

31. What special care should be taken with regard to keeping a cellar clean?

The walls and floor should be free from moisture, and any accumulation whatever of dust or refuse. There should be not only some means of constant ventilation, but the windows ought frequently to be opened to full currents of air from without. *Vegetables should never be allowed to decay in the cellar.* In these days of furnaces, when, in addition to the ordinary upward travel of cellar odors, the sides of the registers in the rooms above afford a direct means of ascent for all the foul or stagnant air that may lurk below, the basement should be the sweetest and most immaculate portion of the house.

32. How is the air strained as it passes into the lungs?

The constant motion of the cilia, which line the air-passages, produces an outward current, which arrests and expels intrusive particles that, swept inward by the breath, would otherwise pass into the lungs.

33. Can one really "draw the air into his lungs"?
(See *Physiology*, p. 80.)

Strictly speaking, no. In the act of inspiration we so contract the muscles as to enlarge the cavity of the chest, thus reducing the pressure upon the lungs, upon which the external atmosphere, in seeking an equilibrium, rushes in to fill the space.

34. How often do we breathe?

Ordinarily about eighteen times a minute.

35. Describe some approved method of ventilation.
(See *Physiology*, p. 02.)

36. What is at once the floor of the chest and the roof of the abdomen?

The diaphragm.

37. What would you do in case of apparent death by drowning or by coal-gas?
(See *Physiology*, p. 264.)

38. What would you do in case of croup, while the doctor was coming?
(See *Physiology*, p. 260.)

39. How would you treat a severe burn?
(See *Physiology*, p. 257.)

40. Describe the various ways in which the water in a well is liable to become unwholesome.

In towns and cities organic matter, solid or in solution, permeates the soil to the depth of several feet, and shallow wells are therefore quite certain to be polluted, as any earth used constantly as a filter will, in the course of years, lose its purifying properties. Wells, too, are often placed in dangerous proximity to cemeteries, cess-pools, barn-yards, vaults, etc., and in many cases receive direct drainage from these pestilential sources. Impurities will collect in wells that are not periodically cleaned, especially if the water in them is not freely exposed to the oxygen of the air. If one must depend upon wellwater, the safest reliance is upon a deep-driven well.

147—1. *Why does a dry, cold atmosphere favorably affect catarrh?*

It tends to diminish inflammation in the mucous membrane lining the nose and nasal passages.

2. *Why should we put on extra covering when we lie down to sleep?*

The respiration and the circulation are then less active. The fire in our corporeal stoves being low, we need extra covering to preserve the warmth of the body.

3. *Is it well to throw off our coats or shawls when we come in heated from a long walk?*

No. We need, instead, to put on extra clothing at such times to keep the body from cooling too rapidly. The best hygienic teachers commend the throwing of a shawl about the shoulders whenever we sit down to rest after fatiguing labor.

4. *Why are close-fitting collars or neck-ties injurious?*

They impede both respiration and circulation.

5. *Which side of the heart is the more liable to inflammation?*

The left; because that contains the red blood just oxygenated in the lungs.

6. *What gives the toper his red nose?*

(See *Physiology*, p. 126.)

The congested state of the capillaries.

7. *Why does not the arm die when the surgeon ties the principal artery leading to it?*

The anastomoses of the arteries enable a collateral circulation to be established, whereby blood is supplied to the arm.

8. *When a fowl is angry, why does its comb redden?*

Because an extra quantity of blood is thrown into that part of the body.

9. *Why does a fat man endure cold better than a lean one?*

Fat is a good non-conductor of heat, and helps to preserve the uniform temperature of the body.

10. *Why does one become thin during a long sickness?*

By absorption, the fat of the body is taken up and used to supply the wants of the system. The old flesh being renewed with new, vigorous material, a person often has better health after such a wasting sickness than previous to it.

11. *What would you do if you should come home "wet to the skin"?*

One should (1) go into a warm room; (2) remove all wet garments; (3) if chilled, take a hot, full or foot bath, and by gentle friction restore the circulation; (4) put on dry clothing.

12. *When the cold air strikes the face, why does it first blanch and then flush?*

The muscles and blood-vessels of the surface are contracted by the cold, and the blood is driven back toward the heart. The reaction which ensues forces the blood again toward the skin, and this flushes with the incoming tide. The face is therefore first whitened and then reddened.

13. *What must be the effect of tight lacing upon the circulation of the blood?*

It must, by contracting the blood-vessels, impede the flow of the blood, and by decreasing the quantity furnished the various organs, injure their action. Thus, finally, it will impair the quality of the blood.

14. *Do you know the position of the large arteries in the limbs, so that in case of accident you could stop the flow of blood?*

These can be located by examining the cut in *Physiology*, page 104, or any good chart of the circulation.

15. When a person is said to be "good-hearted," is it a physical truth?

The expressions, large-hearted, good-hearted, etc., are remains of the old idea that the affections are located in the heart rather than in the brain—the seat of the mind and all its attributes.*

16. Why does a hot foot-bath often relieve the headache?
(See *Physiology*, p. 126.)

It withdraws blood from the head, and so relieves the congested state of that organ.

17. Why does the body of a drowned or strangled person turn blue?

---

* In connection with this subject, the following from a recent article by Dr. Wm. A. Hammond, will be found of interest: "In the very earliest times of which we have any record, and even at the present day among barbarous nations, the idea existed that the brain was not the only organ concerned in the production of mind. ... Doubtless, its origin was due to the fact that, under the influence of certain emotions, there are disturbances in the organs with which they are associated. Thus, love quickens the action of the heart; mental depression or anger deranges the liver; and pity produces what is sometimes called 'a sinking feeling' at the pit of the stomach. It has been customary with modern writers to regard these disturbances as being the effects of emotions that originated in the brain, and not as indicating that the organs in which they are felt have any thing to do with the evolution of love, or anger, or fear, or compassion, or any other passion or feeling. ... The idea has become so widely spread among educated persons that the brain is the only organ of the body that has any direct relation as a generator with the mind, that it seems like a tremendous blow at the system of existing facts to attempt to take from it any of its power. But it is only recently that physiologists and pathologists are beginning to make a thorough investigation into that great division of the nervous system consisting of the sympathetic nerves and their ganglia. ...... Now, it is not unreasonable to suppose that these masses of the tissue in question, that are placed around the heart, the liver, the spine, and other organs, and in vast number in their substance, have some influence in causing the production of those emotions that make themselves felt in the parts of the body with which former universal beliefs, and our present forms of speech, have associated them. We find, too, as an additional fact in support of this view, that in certain mental affections, characterized by great emotional disturbances, these ganglia are in various parts of the body the seats of disease."

The blood is not purified in the lungs, and so blue or venous blood fills the vessels.

18. What are the little "kernels" in the arm-pits?
(See *Physiology*, p. 125.)

They are the lymphatic glands, which sometimes become swollen.

19. When we are excessively warm, would the thermometer show any rise of temperature in the body?
(See *Physiology*, p. 120, note.)

Probably not. In health, the average temperature of the body does not vary more than two degrees.

20. What forces besides that of the heart aid in propelling the blood?
(See FLINT's *Physiology*—The Circulation; CUTLER's *Analytic Anatomy*, etc. p. 166, *et seq*.)

The elasticity of the arteries and the veins, the force of capillary attraction in the capillaries, etc.

21. Why can the pulse be best felt in the wrist?

It is, in general, a mere matter of convenience. We can feel it not only in the radial artery at the wrist, but in the carotid of the neck, the temporal of the forehead, the popliteal* in the inner side of the knee, etc.

22. Why are starving people exceedingly sensitive to any jar?

The marrow of the bones is absorbed, and hence the shock of a jar is unbroken. The nervous system is also weakened by the general prostration.

23. Why will friction, an application of horse-radish leaves, or a blister relieve internal congestion?

They bring the blood to the surface of the body, and so relieve the internal organ.

---

* If the hollow of the knee of one leg be allowed to rest upon the knee of the other one, it may be remarked that the point of the suspended foot moves visibly up and down at each beat of the pulse.

24. Why are students very liable to cold feet?

Because the tendency of the blood is toward the head, to supply the waste in that part of the body.

25. Is the proverb that "blood is thicker than water" literally true?

(See DRAPER's *Human Physiology*, p. 112.)

The specific gravity of the blood varies from 1.050 to 1.059.

26. What is the effect upon the circulation of "holding the breath"?

The blood is not oxygenated, the products of waste accumulate in the system, the circulation is impeded, the blood-vessels become distended, and are liable to burst, while all the delicate organs, especially the brain, are oppressed by congestion.

27. Which side of the heart is the stronger?

The left, which drives the blood to the extremities.

28. How is the heart itself nourished?

The coronary arteries springing from the aorta just after its origin, carry blood to the muscular walls of the heart: the venous blood comes back through the coronary veins, and empties directly into the right auricle.

29. Does any venous blood reach the heart without coming through the venæ cavæ?

(See Question 28.)

30. What would you do, in the absence of a surgeon, in the case of a severe wound?

(See *Physiology*, pp. 128, 258.)

31. What would you do in case of a fever?

(See *Physiology*, p. 263.)

32. What is the most injurious effect of alcohol upon the blood?

(See *Physiology*, p. 144.)

Its action upon the red corpuscles.

33. Are our bodies the same from day to day?

No, they are constantly changing.

34. Show how life comes by death.
(See *Physiology*, p. 122.)

35. Is not the truth just stated as applicable to moral and intellectual as to physical life?

Yes. We increase our moral and intellectual strength in proportion as we use those powers.

36. What vein begins and ends with capillaries?
(See *Physiology*, p. 161.)

The portal vein, which begins with capillaries in the digestive organs, and ends with the same kind of vessels in the liver.

37. By what process is alcohol always formed? Does it exist in nature?

By the process of fermentation. It has been generally believed not to exist in nature, but recent experiments have seemed to indicate that it does so exist, though in extremely minute quantities. "Professor Müntz, of the National Agronomic Institute, in Paris, has, by refined chemical tests, discovered evidences of alcohol in cultivated soils, in rain water, in sea and river water, and in the atmosphere. . . . It appears probable that the alcohol originates in the soil, from the fermentation of the organic matters in it, and is thence diffused as vapor in the atmosphere."—W. O. ATWATER, *Century Magazine*, May, 1888.

38. What percentage of alcohol is contained in the different kinds of liquor?

Ale and porter contain from six to eight per cent.; wine, from seven to seventeen per cent.; brandy and whiskey, from forty to fifty per cent.

39. Does cider possess the same intoxicating principle as brandy?

Yes, because cider that has begun to ferment contains alcohol, which is the intoxicating principle in all spirituous drinks.

40. Describe the general properties of alcohol.

It is volatile, antiseptic, a solvent. It burns without smoke, and with great heat, and has a remarkable affinity for water. It boils at 172° Fahr.

41. Show that alcohol is a narcotic poison.
(See answer to Question 42.)

42. If alcohol is not a stimulant, how does it cause the heart to overwork?

Recently, physiological research has served to explain the reason why, under alcohol, the heart at first beats so quickly, why the pulses rise, and why the minute blood-vessels become so strongly injected.

At one time it was imagined that alcohol acts immediately upon the heart, by stimulating it to increased motion; and from this idea—false idea, I should say—of the primary action of alcohol, many erroneous conclusions have been drawn. We have now learned that there exist many chemical bodies which act in the same manner as alcohol, and that their effect is not to stimulate the heart, but to weaken the contractile force of the extreme and minute vessels which the heart fills with blood at each of its strokes. These bodies produce, in fact, a paralysis of the organic nervous supply of the vessels which constitute the minute vascular structures. The minute vessels when paralyzed offer inefficient resistance to the force of the heart, and the pulsating organ thus liberated, like the main-spring of a clock from which the resistance has been removed, quickens in action, dilating the feebly-resistant vessels, and giving evidence really not of increased, but of wasted power.—B. W. RICHARDSON.

43. Why is the skin of a drunkard always red and blotched?

It is the effect of alcoholic action on the vascular structure.

44. What danger is there in occasionally using alcoholic drinks?

Aside from injurious temporary effects, there is always the supreme danger of forming a habit which will become uncontrollable.

45. What is meant by a fatty degeneration of the heart?
(See *Physiology*, p. 143.)

In this disease, fat is substituted for true muscular tissue.

46. What keeps the blood in circulation between the beats of the heart?

The blood starts with a rush from the heart by the force of its action; the expansion and contraction of the arteries, into which it is thus powerfully propelled, impart a steady onward pressure, which sends it to the capillaries; there the processes of oxidation, nutrition, and secretion draw the current onward, and push it out toward the veins; thence it is forced back to the heart by the power originated in the capillaries. (See Draper's *Human Physiology*, large edition, p. 145.)

47. What is the office of the capillaries?
(See *Physiology*, p. 373, note.)

48. Does alcohol interfere with this function?
(See *Physiology*, p. 117, note.)

Alcohol sometimes causes the red corpuscles to adhere in masses, which obstruct their passage through the tiny capillary tubes.

49. How does alcohol interfere with the regular office of the membranes?
(See *Physiology*, p. 143.)

It absorbs their moisture, and causes them to become dry, hard, and thick.

50. How does it check the process of oxidation?
(See *Physiology*, pp. 145, 146.)

By its effect upon the red blood-corpuscles, destroying their efficiency as oxygen-carriers.

¶ 87—1. How do clothing and shelter economize food?

The force which would be converted into heat to preserve the temperature of the body, is saved. The food needed to supply this amount of force may be reserved or changed into flesh, or into other forms of force.

2. Is it well to take a long walk before breakfast?
(See *Physiology*, p. 41.)

A vigorous person in good health and in a healthy region

may do so, but one in ill health, or in a malarious district, needs to be braced with food before taking any except very light exercise.

3. *Why is warm food easier to digest than cold?*

Heat favors the chemical change whereby the food is prepared for assimilation.

4. *Why is salt beef less nutritious than fresh?*
(See *Physiology*, p. 187, note.)

The salts and juices of the meat are extracted by the brine.

5. *What should be the food of a man recovering from a fever?*

It should be that which is nutritious, easily digested, and not over-stimulating. Beef-tea or essence* is generally commended. As soon as the patient will bear it, beefsteak, tender, broiled, and not overdone, is most beneficial.

6. *Is a cup of black coffee a healthful close to a hearty dinner?*

The tannic acid contained in tea and coffee is neutralized by the milk generally used with these beverages. In *café noir*, black or clear coffee, the tannic acid acts unfavorably on the mucous membrane lining the stomach. Besides, the coffee, like a dessert, is superfluous, the appetite being already satisfied. It therefore tends, both actively and negatively, to delay the digestion of the meal. The glass of wine sometimes taken to aid digestion merely deadens the sensibility of the stomach, so that the food is hurried, half-digested, out into the intestines.†

---

* Dr. Martindale gives the following recipe for making this essence: Cut a quantity of lean beef into small pieces, put it into a strong bottle, without water, cork it loosely, so that the steam can escape, and immerse the bottle to its neck in a vessel of cold water. Place on the fire, and boil for two hours; then pour off the essence.

† Mix some bread and meat with gastric juice; place them in a vial, and keep that vial in a sand-bath at the slow heat of 98 degrees, occasionally shaking briskly the contents, to imitate the motion of the stomach; you will find, after six or eight hours, the whole contents blended into one

7. Should iced water be used at a meal?

Only a person in robust health can endure the shock of drinking iced water at a meal. Indeed, drinking of iced water under any circumstances is dangerous and hurtful. If used at all, it should be carefully and *slowly sipped*, a little at a time.

8. Why is strong tea or coffee injurious?

The tannic acid acts unfavorably on the coatings of the stomach.* The nervous system is over-stimulated, and, when the reaction occurs, becomes correspondingly depressed and weakened. The constant decay of the body, so essential to its highest activity, is greatly retarded. Wakefulness is often induced, and thus the organs are deprived of that rest which is absolutely necessary for perfect health.

9. Should food or drink be taken hot?

The pepsin of the gastric juice, in order to produce its effect, must have a moderately warm temperature, neither too hot nor too cold. The gastric juice will not act upon the food when near the freezing point of water, neither will it have any effect if raised to the neighborhood of a boiling temperature. It must be intermediate between the two; and its greatest activity is about 100 degrees Fahrenheit, which is exactly the temperature of the interior of the living stomach.—DALTON'S *Physiology*, p. 103.

10. Are fruit-cakes, rich pastry, and puddings wholesome?

(See BLACK'S *Ten Laws of Health*, p. 83, *et seq.*)

They are too concentrated. They are not easily penetrated by the juices of the system, and hence are not quickly digested. They stimulate the appetite, and so lead to gluttony. They supply the system with an over-abundance of nutrition, for

pultaceous mass. If to another vial of food and gastric juice, treated in the same way, you add a glass of pale ale or a quantity of alcohol, at the end of seven or eight hours, or even some days, the food is scarcely acted upon at all.

*Tea contains from 14 to 16 per cent. of this astringent substance, and coffee not over 6 per cent.—YOUMANS.

which the blood has no use, and so lead to biliousness and other diseases of the blood and digestive organs.

11. Why are warm biscuit and bread hard of digestion?

They form a pasty mass, which the juices of the digestive organs penetrate very slowly.

12. Should any stimulants be used in youth?

No. The system is then vigorous, and all its functions promptly performed. If stimulants are ever used, it should be when the body needs forcing, as when recovering from disease, or languid with the decay of the natural powers in old age.

13. Why should bread be made spongy?
(See Question 11.)

14. Which should remain longer in the mouth, bread or meat?

Bread, since the pepsin is essential to the conversion of starch into sugar.

15. Why should cold water be used in making soup, and hot in boiling meat?

In the former case, we desire to extract the juices of the meat; in the latter, to retain them by quickly coagulating the albumen on the surface of the meat.

16. Name the injurious effects of over-eating.
(See *Physiology*, p. 176.)

17. Why do not buckwheat cakes, with syrup and butter, taste as well in July as in January?

In tne winter, the system craves highly carbonaceous food; in the summer, it relishes cooling, acid drinks, and an unstimulating diet.

18. Why is a late supper injurious?

The system is wearied with the day's labor, and the stomacn is unfitted to undertake the task of digesting a meal as much as the body is to begin a new day's task unrefreshed by sleep.*

*Being allowed for once to speak, I would take the opportunity to set forth how ill, in all respects, we stomachs are used. From the beginning to the end of life, we are either afflicted with too little or too much, or not the right thing, or things which are horribly disagreeable to us; or are otherwise thrown into a state of discomfort. I do not think it proper to take up a moment in bewailing the Too Little, for that is an evil which is never the fault of our masters, but rather the result of their misfortunes; and, indeed, we would sometimes feel as if it were a relief from other kinds of distress if we were put upon short allowance for a few days. But we conceive ourselves to have matter for serious complaint against mankind in respect of the Too Much, which is always an evil voluntarily incurred. What a pity that in the progress of discovery we can not establish some means of a good understanding between mankind and their stomachs; for really the effects of their non-acquaintance are most vexatious. Human beings seem to be, to this day, completely in the dark as to what they ought to take at any time, and err almost as often from ignorance as from depraved appetite. Sometimes, for instance, when we of the inner house are rather weakly, they will send us down an article that we could deal with when only in a state of robust health. Sometimes, when we would require a mild vegetable diet, they will persist in the most stimulating and irritating of viands.

What sputtering we poor stomachs have when mistakes of that kind occur! What remarks we indulge in regarding our masters! "What's this, now?" will one of us say; "ah, detestable stuff! What a ridiculous fellow that man is! Will he never learn? Just the very thing I did not want. If he would only send down a bowl of fresh leek soup or barley broth, there would be some sense in it"; and so on. If we had only been allowed to give the slightest hint now and then, like faithful servants as we are, from how many miseries might we have saved both our masters and ourselves!

I have been a stomach for about forty years, during all of which time I have endeavored to do my duty faithfully and punctually. My master, however, is so reckless, that I would defy any stomach of ordinary ability and capacity to get along pleasantly with him. The fact is, like almost all other men, he, in his eating and drinking, considers his own pleasure only, and never once reflects on the poor wretch who has to be responsible for the disposal of every thing down-stairs. Scarcely on any day does he fail to exceed the strict rule of temperance; nay, there is scarcely a single meal which is altogether what it ought to be. My life is therefore one of continual worry and fret; I am never allowed to rest from morning till night, and have not a moment in the four-and-twenty hours that I can safely call my own. My greatest trial takes place in the evening, when my master has dined. If you only saw what a mess this

19. What makes a man "bilious"?

(See HALL's *Health by Good Living*, p. 111, *et seq*.)

The liver strains the bile out of the blood. This waste matter is not withdrawn when the liver is inactive, and hence the face and eyes become yellow—the color of bile, and the functions all become torpid.

said dinner is—soup, fish, flesh, fowl, ham, rice, potatoes, table-beer, sherry, tart, pudding, cheese, bread, all mixed up together. I am accustomed to the thing, so don't feel much shocked; but my master himself would faint at the sight. The slave of duty in all circumstances, I call in my friend Gastric Juice, and we set to work with as much good-will as if we had the most agreeable task in the world before us. But, unluckily, my master has an impression very firmly fixed upon him that our business is apt to be vastly promoted by an hour or two's drinking; so he continues at table among his friends, and pours down some bottle and a half of wine, perhaps of various sorts, that bothers Gastric Juice and me to a degree which no one can have any idea of. In fact, this wine undoes our work almost as fast as we do it, besides blinding and poisoning us poor servants into the bargain. On many occasions I am obliged to give up my task for the time altogether; for while this vinous shower is going on I would defy the most vigorous stomach in the world to make any advance in its business worth speaking of. Sometimes things go to a much greater length than at others: and my master will paralyze us in this manner for hours, not always, indeed, with wine, but occasionally with punch, one ingredient of which—the lemon—is particularly odious to us. All this time I can hear him jollifying away at a great rate, drinking health to his neighbors, and ruining his own.

I am a lover of early hours, as are my brethren generally. To this we are very much disposed by the extremely hard work which we usually undergo during the day. About ten o'clock, having, perhaps, at that time got all our labors past, and feeling fatigued and exhausted, we like to sink into repose, not to be again disturbed till next morning at breakfast-time. Well, how it may be with others I can't tell; but so it is, that my master never scruples to rouse me up from my first sleep, and give me charge of an entirely new meal, after I thought I was to be my own master for the night. This is a hardship of the most grievous kind. Only imagine me, after having gathered in my coal, drawn on my night-cap, and gone to bed, called up and made to take charge of a quantity of stuff which I know I shall not be able to get off my hands all night! Such, O mankind, are the woes which befall our tribe in consequence of your occasionally yielding to the temptations of "a little supper." I see turkey and tongue in grief and terror. Macaroni fills me with frantic alarm. I behold jelly and trifle follow in mute despair. O that I had the power of standing beside my master, and holding his unreflecting hand, as he thus prepares for

20. What is the best remedy?

Diet to give the organs rest, and active exercise to arouse the secretions and the circulation.

21. What is the practical use of hunger?

To prompt us to furnish the body with sufficient food.

22. How can jugglers drink when standing on their heads?

Because water does not fall into the stomach by its own weight, but is conveyed thither from the mouth by the contraction of the muscular bands of the œsophagus.

23. Why do we relish butter on bread?

Butter supplies the carbonaceous element in which bread is lacking.

my torment and his own! Here, too, the old mistaken notion about the need of something stimulating besets him, and down comes a deluge of hot spirits and water, that causes me to writhe in agony, and almost sends Gastric Juice off in the sulks to bed. Nor does the infatuated man rest here. If the company be agreeable, one glass follows another, while I am kept standing, as it were, with my sleeves tucked up, ready to begin, but unable to perform a single stroke of work.

I feel that the strength which I ought to have at my present time of life has passed from me. I am getting weak, and peevish, and evil-disposed. A comparatively small trouble sits long and sore upon me. Bile, from being my servant, is becoming my master; and a bad one he makes, as all good servants ever do. I see nothing before me but a premature old age of pains and groans, and gripes and grumblings, which will, of course, not last over long; and thus I shall be cut short in my career, when I should have been enjoying life's tranquil evening, without a single vexation of any kind to trouble me. Were I of a revengeful temper, it might be a consolation to think that my master—the cause of all my woes—must suffer and sink with me; but I don't see how this can mend my own case; and, from old acquaintance, I am rather disposed to feel sorry for him, as one who has been more ignorant and imprudent than ill-meaning. In the same spirit let me hope that this true and unaffected account of my case may prove a warning to other persons how they use their stomachs; for, they may depend upon it, whatever injustice they do to *us*, in their days of health and pride, will be repaid to *themselves* in the long-run—our friend Madame Nature being a remarkably accurate accountant, who makes no allowance for ignorance or mistakes.—CHAMBERS' *Memoir of a Stomach*.

24. What would you do if you had taken arsenic by mistake?

(See *Physiology*, p. 265.)

25. Why should ham and sausage be thoroughly cooked?

The trichina, which frequents pork, is only destroyed at a high temperature.

26. Why do we wish butter on fish, eggs with tapioca, oil on salad, and milk with rice?

To supply the elements of food lacking in the composition of fish, tapioca, etc.

27. Explain the relation of food to exercise.

Their relation is exceedingly intimate. If we eat much we should take more exercise, and if, on the contrary, we labor more, we desire additional food. Violent exercise, directly after a hearty meal, is injurious; but a gentle, quiet half-hour's saunter will greatly benefit the digestion.

28. How do you explain the difference in the manner of eating between carnivorous and herbivorous animals?

Meat requires less saliva to aid in its digestion, and hence it is mainly digested in the stomach; while vegetable food needs to be thoroughly masticated and incorporated with the salivary mucus.

29. Why is a child's face plump and an old man's wrinkled?

In the child the processes of nutrition are more active than those of waste. The reverse is the case in old age.

30. Show how life depends on repair and waste.

(See *Popular Chemistry*, p. 19, et seq.; and *Physiology*, p. 122.)

31. What is the difference between the decay of the teeth and the constant decay of the body?

The particles of the teeth lost by decay are not renewed, while in the body they are replaced as fast as worn out. The soundness of teeth is often affected by the general health. It has been said that a man who can preserve his teeth till he is fifty years old may count on keeping them through life.

32. Should biscuit and cake containing yellow spots of soda be eaten?

Certainly not. The alkali neutralizes the acids of the alimentary juices, and thus impairs their functions, while it corrodes and irritates the delicate mucous lining of the digestive organs.

33. Tell how the body is composed of organs, how organs are made up of tissues, and how tissues consist of cells.
(See *Physiology*, p. 175, note.)

34. Why do we not need to drink three pints of water per day?
(See *Physiology*, p. 151.)

The amount of water one needs depends upon the character of his food, the nature of his labor, and the activity of the three eliminating organs—the skin, the kidneys, and the lungs. One perspiring freely, or eating dry food, needs more drink than one whose skin is inactive, or whose food consists, in part, of soups or watery vegetables.

35. Why, during a pestilence, are those who use liquors as a beverage the first, and often the only victims?

The nervous system has become impaired, the digestion weakened, and the blood impoverished; hence, the functions of the body being disturbed, its ability to resist disease is greatly lessened.

36. What two secretions seem to have the same general use?

The saliva and the pancreatic juice both change starch into sugar. They have other important uses, however, in the process of digestion. The former softens the food and aids in the work of mastication, while the latter emulsifies the fats.

37. How may the digestive organs be strengthened?

The digestive organs, like the other organs, are strengthened by judicious labor. The stomach is a muscle, and, like muscle generally, grows strong by use and weak by disuse. The same laws should govern one in his daily exercise of every organ—brain, hand, and stomach.

38. Is the old rule, "after dinner sit awhile," a good one?

Yes; a certain period of rest, after a hearty meal, assists the process of digestion.

39. What would you do if you had taken laudanum by mistake? Paris green? Sugar of lead? Oxalic acid? Phosphorus from matches? Ammonia? Corrosive sublimate?

(See *Physiology*, p. 266.)

40. What is the simplest way to produce vomiting, so essential in case of accidental poisoning?

If mustard is at hand, mix a little thoroughly with warm water, and drink immediately; if mustard is not convenient, warm soap-suds will do; if neither is within reach, the finger thrust gently down the throat may serve the purpose till other means can be procured, or medical aid arrives.

41. In what way does alcohol interfere with the digestion?

"Alcohol in certain quantities will harden meat, and thereby interfere with its digestion; it will further precipitate pepsin and peptones; and in large quantities it will also stop the secretion of gastric juice, increase the secretion of mucus, and even lead to vomiting."

42. Is alcohol assimilated?

(See *Physiology*, p. 178.)

No.

43. What is the effect of alcohol on the albuminous substances?

Pure brandy held in the mouth a short time will cause a burning sensation, and the inside of the cheek will become slightly whitened and corrugated. This effect is due to the albuminous substances in the mucous membrane being partly coagulated by the alcohol, and it illustrates the action of this agent upon the tissues.

44. Is there any nourishment in beer?

The following table will show at a glance the materials required for, and the result of, brewing:

Materials.	Chief Compounds in Beer.
Malt.	Alcohol, or spirits of wine, from 3 to 8 per cent.
Water.	Dextrine, about 4.5 per cent.
Hops.	Albuminoids, 0.5 "
Yeast from a previous brewing.	Sugar, 0.5 "
	Acetic and succinic acids, 0.3 per cent.
	Carbonic acid, 0.15 per cent.
	Mineral matter, 0.3 "

Here it is seen that the nutriment of the malt has been converted into the stimulant—alcohol. Whatever nourishment there may be is of a saccharine nature, the dextrine when in the stomach becoming converted into sugar. Of the two necessary nourishing elements—the nitrogenous and the carbonaceous—the former is practically wanting; and of the latter there is not enough to justify the use of malt liquor for the sake of it. The chief difference between porters or stouts, and ales, consists in the malt from which the former is made, having been more highly dried.—*London Medical Temperance Journal.*

45. Show how the excessive use of alcohol may first increase and afterward decrease the size of the liver.

In the case of cirrhosis (sometimes called gin-drinker's liver), the liver first becomes enlarged from exudation into the connective tissue. After a time, this becomes organized into fibrous tissues, and these fibrous bands contract and press together the blood-vessels and cells of the liver, until both become atrophied and ultimately destroyed. In this way the organ becomes much smaller in size, and greatly reduced in weight.

46. Will liquor help one to endure cold and exposure?

(See *Physiology*, p. 183.)

No. Experiments with Arctic voyagers have abundantly proved this, while the certainty that alcohol, in its secondary effect, lowers the temperature of the body, places the fact beyond dispute.

47. What is a fatty degeneration of the kidneys?
(See *Physiology*, p. 181.)

48. Contrast the action of alcohol and water in the body.
(See *Physiology*, p. 178, note.)

49. Is alcohol, in any proper sense of the term, a food?

This is a mooted point between the defenders and the opposers of alcoholic drinks. The author of this Manual considers that the weight of argument and the preponderance of eminent authorities justify a decided "No" to this question.

50. Does liquor strengthen the muscles of a working-man?
(See *Physiology*, p. 183.)

On the contrary, the strength of muscle is directly impaired. Dr. Parkes, an eminent English physician, tested this in a practical way. Taking a certain number of working-men of similar age, equal health, and provided with the same amount of food, he divided them into two gangs, agreeing to pay them wages in proportion to work performed. The first gang he supplied with a daily ration of drink, but withheld it from the second. During the first hour or two the "alcoholic gang" went decidedly ahead of the other. Then they began to flag, while the "non-alcoholics" went steadily on, and before the day was done had far outstripped the drinkers. He then reversed the experiment, giving the second gang an alcoholic ration, and withholding it from the first. The result was the same—the non-drinkers always coming out ahead. So decided was the result of the experiment, and so deeply did it impress the men who were engaged in it, though they were not aware of its full significance, that the alcohol men begged to be put upon the non-alcohol gang, in order, as they expressed it, that they "might make a little more money."

51. Is liquor a wholesome "tonic"?

Certainly not a "wholesome" tonic, nor a true "tonic" in any sense, for the reasons elaborated in the answers to the previous questions. A real tonic builds up the system, and puts it upon a permanent basis of healthy function. The effect of alcohol is to impair, not to build up.

52. Is it a good plan to take a glass of liquor before dinner?

Alcohol is peculiarly injurious when taken upon an empty stomach, and furnishes a sorry preparation for the proper digestion of food.
(See answers to Questions 42, 43.)

224—*1. Why is the pain of incipient hip-disease frequently felt in the knee?*

The sensation of pain is located by the mind, at the part of the body where the injured nerve takes its rise.

2. Why does a child require more sleep than an aged person?

The processes of nutrition are going on rapidly, and, in youth, much rest is required to repair the losses of each day; in age, waste predominates, and the repairs made are of a temporary character. The building is soon to be torn down, and little effort is taken to beautify or strengthen that which is to be used for so short a time.

3. When you put your finger in the palm of a sleeping child, why will he grasp it?

The unconscious action of the near nervous centers produces a contraction of the muscles.

4. How may we strengthen the brain?

By judicious, habitual, but not exhaustive employment. The life of the brain is in change. Monotony is stagnation, and stagnation is decay.

5. What is the object of pain?

Pain is monitory in its character. It guards against danger and warns us of the presence of *disease*, *i.e.*, the want of ease. Were it not for this, we should lose the use of the more delicate organs. A child might gaze at the sun until its eyesight was ruined. The author knew of a man who had lost the sense of feeling in one leg because of the sensory nerve being severed. He was constantly bruising and burning that limb until he ruined it entirely.

6. *Why will a blow on the stomach sometimes stop the heart?*

By sympathy. The pneumogastric or tenth pair of nerves supply the stomach and the heart.

7. *How long will it take for the brain of a man six feet high to receive news of an injury to his foot, and to reply?*

The nervous force has been estimated to travel at the rate of one hundred feet per second, although authorities vary much. Taking this figure, it would require about one eighth of a second.*

8. *How can we grow beautiful?*

If one is penurious, selfish, or hard-hearted, his face will betray the fact to every passer-by. Purity of thought and nobleness of soul, the simple habit of cherishing high and generous purposes, refine and spiritualize the countenance, making, at last, the homeliest features to glow with a beauty that will be a true "joy forever."

9. *Why do intestinal worms sometimes affect a child's sight?*

Through the action of the sympathetic system of nerves.

10. *Is there any indication of character in physiognomy?*

(See Question 8; also *Physiology*, p. 205.)

11. *When one's finger is burned, where is the ache?*

All pain is in the brain. It is located, however, by the mind, at the place of the injury.

---

* A barefooted boy steps on a thorn. If he had to wait for news of the injury to be sent to his brain, and an order to be telegraphed back to remove the foot, much time would be lost. As it is, with the first prick the nearer nerve-centers act and order the foot off almost before the brain has heard of the accident.

12. Is a seldom-opened parlor likely to be a healthy room?

No. It is generally ill-ventilated, and, to preserve the furniture, kept dark, and hence damp.

13. Why can an idle scholar read his lesson and at the same time count the marbles in his pocket?
(See *Physiology*, p. 204, note.)

The duality of the brain may, perhaps, account for this.

14. In amputating a limb, what part, when divided, will cause the keenest pain?

When a surgical operation is performed, the most painful part of it is the incision through the skin; the muscles, cartilage, and bone being comparatively without sensation. Hence, if we could benumb the surface, certain of the lesser operations might be undergone without great inconvenience. This is, in fact, very successfully accomplished by means of the cold produced by throwing a spray of ether, or of some other rapidly evaporating liquid, upon the part to be cut.

15. What is the effect of bad air on nervous people?

The nerves connect all the organs of the body. They are therefore especially sensitive to a derangement in the function of any organ. Bad air causes impure blood, deranged nutrition, and hence a disturbance of the entire economy.

16. Is there any truth in the proverb that "he who sleeps, dines"?

The proverb expresses the fact that the nourishment of the brain and other parts goes on actively during sleep, they being controlled by the sympathetic nerves.

17. What does a high, wide forehead indicate?

It suggests a large brain and a high intellectual power.

18. How does indigestion frequently cause a headache?

Through the action of the sympathetic system.

19. What is the cause of one's foot being "asleep"?
(See *Physiology*, p. 225, note.)

20. When an injury to the nose has been remedied by transplanting skin from the forehead, why is a touch to the former felt in the latter?

The mind refers the sensation to the place where the nerve naturally had its origin—*i.e.*, the part over which its tiny fibers were originally distributed.

21. Are closely-curtained windows healthful?

No. They keep out the sun and the fresh air.

22. Why, in falling from a height, do the limbs instinctively take a position to defend the important organs?

The reflex action of the spinal cord moves the limbs into a position of defense, the brain having no time to act.

23. What causes the pylorus to open and close at the right time?

The reflex action of the nerves which preside over that organ. In a similar way, a tickling in the throat excites coughing.

24. Why is pleasant exercise most beneficial?

A chief condition of keeping the brain healthy is to keep the unconscious nervous functions in full vigor, and in natural alternations of activity and repose. Thus it is that (besides its effect in increasing the breathing and the general vigor of the vital processes) muscular exercise has so manifest a beneficial influence on a depressed or irritable state of mind. The bodily movement, by affording an outlet to the activity of the spinal cord, withdraws a source of irritation from the brain; or it may relieve excitement of that organ by carrying off its energy into a safe channel.—HINTON.

25. Why does grief cause one to lose his appetite?

Through the action of the sympathetic system.

26. Why should we never study directly after dinner?

The blood then sets toward the stomach, and the whole strength of the system is needed to properly digest the food.

27. What produces the peristaltic movement of the stomach?

The presence of the food which, through the sympathetic system, acting involuntarily, sets in motion the complicated apparatus of digestion.

28. Why is a healthy child so restless and full of mischief?

Nature prompts it to exercise all the muscles in its body in order to their proper development.

29. Why is a slight blow on the back of a rabbit's neck fatal?

The medulla oblongata is not defended with thick muscles as in man.

30. Why can one walk and carry on a conversation at the same time?

(See Question 13.)

31. What are the dangers of over-study?

(See HINTON's *Health and its Conditions*, p. 193, *et seq.*, and CUTLER's *Analytical Anatomy*, p. 248; also, *Physiology*, p. 331.)

Exhaustive mental labor overstrains the delicate nerve-cells of the brain, and the condition of the blood-vessels of the entire body, especially of the vital organs, is regulated, moment by moment, by its changing moods. Even the supply furnished the brain is subject to the same influence. Hence results deranged nutrition, impaired circulation, and weakened brain and body. Whenever we consume vital energy faster than it can be replaced, we encroach upon the capital, and thus cause an irreparable injury.

32. What is the influence of idleness upon the brain?

If we would have healthy bodies we must have active brains, that the streams of force may flow into every organ from a full, fresh, energizing source. "The perfect health of a man is not that of an ox or a horse." The proper exercise of the brain is an essential element of real life.

33. State the close relation which exists between physical and mental health and disease.

A partial cultivation of the mental faculties is incompatible not only with the highest order of thought, but with the highest degree of health and efficiency. The result of professional experience fairly warrants the statement that in persons of a high grade of intellectual endowment and cultivation, other things being equal, the force of moral shocks is more easily broken, tedious and harassing exercise of particular powers more safely borne, than in those of an opposite description, and disease, when it comes, is more readily controlled and cured. The kind of management which consists in awakening a new order of emotion, in exciting new trains of thought, in turning attention to some new matter of study or speculation, must be far less efficacious, because less applicable, in one whose mind has always had a limited range than in one of larger resources and capacities. In endeavoring to restore the disordered mind of the clod-hopper who has scarcely an idea beyond that of his manual employment, the great difficulty is to find some available point from which conservative influences may be projected. He dislikes reading, he never learned amusements, he feels no interest in the affairs of the world; and, unless the circumstances allow of some kind of bodily labor, his mind must remain in a state of solitary isolation, brooding over its morbid fancies, and utterly incompetent to initiate any recuperative movement.—Dr. RAY.

34. In what consists the value of the power of habit?

It saves the "wear and tear" of our principles. We can perform an act a few times, though with difficulty, and then ever after it becomes a habit. We resist evil once, and thenceforth it is easier to resist. We can become accustomed to do good, so that the chances will all be in favor of our well-being in any emergency. By so much as the power of habit is thus pregnant with good, by so much is it susceptible of terrible evil.

35. How many pairs of nerves supply the eye?
(See *Physiology*, p. 199.)

Three; the motores oculi.

36. Describe the reflex actions in reading aloud.

The body is kept erect, the hand holds the book, the eyes are directed to the page, the vocal organs pronounce the words, the features express the sentiments, and the other hand makes corresponding gestures—yet all the time the mind is intent only upon the thought conveyed.

37. Under what circumstances does paralysis occur?

When the nerve leading to any part of the body is injured or fails to keep up communications between that portion and the mind.

38. If the eyelids of a profound sleeper were raised, and a candle brought near, would the iris contract?

It would, by reflex action.

39. How does one cough in his sleep?

By the reflex action of the near nervous centers. A tickling in the throat, or some other cause, acts as the stimulus to excite their action.

40. Give illustration of the unconscious action of the brain.

(See *Physiology*, p. 225. Read also the article "The Antechamber of Consciousness," in *Popular Science Monthly*, March, 1888.)

41. Is chewing tobacco more injurious than smoking?

It is not only more filthy, but also more detrimental to the health, as a chewer is in danger of swallowing more of the poisonous constituents of tobacco, from the constant and profuse excitation of saliva, which must either be swallowed or conspicuously ejected. As a rule, however, modesty in respect to the disposal of his "tobacco juice" does not hinder the veteran chewer from bestowing his peculiar favors generously and openly, and to the least conscious injury to himself. On the other hand, a smoker, especially a cigarette smoker, is liable to dangerous throat diseases, incurred by the heated smoke inhaled from the cigarette.

42. Ought a man to retire from business while his faculties are still unimpaired?

No. It is always a mistake for a man who has led an active life to withdraw, at once, from all occupation and to resign himself to idleness. A proper degree of functional exercise is as necessary to the perfect health of the mind and the brain as to that of the body.

43. Which is the more exhaustive to the brain, worry or severe mental application?
(See *Physiology*, p. 331.)

Worry is far more exhaustive of the vital forces than the severest mental labor, pursued calmly and dispassionately.

44. Is it a blessing to be beyond the necessity for work?

By no means. On the contrary, the "middle-class people," those who do not suffer from actual bodily want, but who are obliged to work in order to procure luxuries, or even comforts, are proverbially happier than those who are born to riches, and who have no incentive to systematic exertion.

45. Show how anger, hate, and the other degrading passions are destructive to the brain.

The effect of anger upon the brain is to produce first a paralysis, and, afterward, during reaction, a congestion of the vessels of that organ. Passionate people often die suddenly of faintness in the moment of white rage, when the cerebral vessels and the heart are paralyzed. Or they may outlive this first stage, only to succumb to the second, when reactive congestion has led to engorgement of the vessels of the brain, and apoplexy ensues. Intensified hatred acts in a similar manner, but more slowly. The effect on the brain of extreme fear is also akin to that of rage, and may result in sudden death from syncope.

The more common and permanent effect of fear, however, is an intense irritability, followed by doubt, suspicion, and distrust, leading toward or to insanity. From a sudden terror deeply felt, the young mind rarely recovers; never, I believe, if hereditary tendency to insanity be a part of its nature.

Of these three passions, anger stands first as most detrimental to life. He is a man very rich indeed in physical power who can afford to be angry. The richest can not afford it many times without insuring the penalty, a penalty that is always severe. What is still worse of this passion is, that the very disease it engenders feeds it, so that if the impulse go many times unchecked it becomes the master of the man.—B. W. RICHARDSON.

46. Are not amusements, to repair the waste of the nervous energy, especially needed by persons whose life is one of care and toil?

Yes, cheerful recreation is necessary in proportion to the severity of toil and care. Nothing will replenish heavily-assessed brain capital like occasional rollicking merriment.

47. Is not severe mental labor incompatible with a rapidly-growing body?

Decidedly. A rapidly-growing child should never be overburdened with mental labor. Youthful prodigies seldom develop into solid, "level-headed" adults. Every extra demand upon the youthful brain, beyond its normal power of healthy endurance, is subtracted with usury from its future reserve stock.

48. How shall we induce the system to perform all its functions regularly?

By uniformly obeying all the laws of Hygiene.

49. How does alcohol interfere with the action of the nerves?
(See *Physiology*, p. 208.)

Alcohol has the same effect upon the nerve-cells that water or ashes has upon a coal fire. Apply water in small quantity, and your fire will burn more slowly; apply a large enough bucketful, and it will cease to exist. When the cook rakes up the ashes and covers her fire before going to bed, she performs the same physical experiment as her master who soothes his nerves with alcohol before retiring at night. But the cook would be very late with breakfast if she trusted to such a fire to cook the bacon, and the work accomplished by a brain affected by alcohol is both small in quantity and inferior in quality. It is as difficult to send proper messages along a nerve under the influence of alcohol, as it is to fire a train of damp gunpowder.—J. M. HOWIE.

50. *What is the general effect of alcohol upon the character?*

(See *Physiology*, p. 212.)

Alcohol exalts and excites the animal centers; it lets loose the passions, and gives them more or less of unlicensed domination over the whole man. "From the beginning to the end of its influence it subdues reason and sets free passion. The analogies, physical and mental, are perfect. That which loosens the tension of the vessels which feed the body with due order of precision, and thereby lets loose the heart to violent excess of unbridled motion, loosens also the reason and lets loose the passions. In both instances, heart and head are for a time out of harmony—their balance is broken. The destructive effects of alcohol on the human mind present the saddest picture of its influence. Memory irretrievably lost; words and very elements of speech forgotten, or words displaced to have no meaning in them; rage and anger persistent and mischievous, or remittent and impotent; fear at every corner of life; distrust on every side; grief merged into blank despair, and hopelessness into permanent melancholy. As I have moved among those who are physically stricken with alcohol, and have detected under the various disguises of name the fatal diseases, the pains and penalties it imposes on the body, the picture has been sufficiently cruel. But even that picture pales as I conjure up, without any stretch of imagination, the devastations which the same agent inflicts on the mind."—RICHARDSON.

51. *Does alcohol tend to produce clearness and vigor of thought?*

(See *Physiology*, p. 212.)

Quite the reverse. Its effect upon the brain and nervous system is strikingly opposed to clearness of judgment and logical reasoning. See answer to preceding Question.

52. *What is the general effect of alcohol on the muscles?*

They lose their nervous control, because of the enfeebling of the nervous stimulus. The muscles of the lower lip usually fail first; then the muscles of the lower limbs, the extensor muscles giving way earlier than the flexors. As they come still more under the depressing influence of the paralyzing agent, their structure becomes temporarily deranged, and their contractile power reduced.

53. Does alcohol have any effect on the bones? The skin?

As the bones are nourished by the blood, whatever materially impoverishes the blood must affect the bones.

The oft-repeated temporary relaxations of the vessels of the skin, resulting from alcoholic potations, ultimately become chronic, and certain parts, such as the nose and cheek, assume a distinctive appearance of confirmed vascular relaxation. From this deficient tonicity of the skin-vessels, the cutaneous secretion becomes irregular; perspiration becomes abnormally profuse, and sometimes is extremely acid; and, finally, swollen eruptions and scaly blotches ensue.

54. What is the cause of the alcoholic chill?

(See *Physiology*, p. 210.)

55. Show how alcohol tends to develop man's lower rather than his higher nature.

(See answer to Question 50.)

56. When we wish really to strengthen the brain, should we use alcohol?

(See *Physiology*, p. 210; also, answer to Question 50.)

Never.

57. Why is alcohol used to preserve anatomical specimens?

Because of its antiseptic properties. These were well known in ancient times, and palm wine was used by the Egyptians in their most costly processes of embalming the dead.

58. What is meant by an inherited taste for liquor?
(See *Physiology*, p. 185.)

59. Ought a person to be punished for a crime committed during intoxication?

Yes; because he knows in taking the alcoholic poison into his system what the logical effect will be upon his actions. At the same time, the rum-seller ought in justice also to receive punishment for the criminal offense of aiding and abetting such a state of moral perversion.

60. Should a boy ever smoke?

Never. Tobacco, in addition to its other evil effects, notably stunts healthy growth.

61. To what extent are we responsible for the health of our body?

To the extent of our neglect of known hygienic rules, or even, in this age of easily-acquired information, to the extent of our lack of knowledge of these rules.

62. Why does alcohol tend to collect in the brain?
(See *Physiology*, p. 210.)

One cause is the great affinity of alcohol for water and the peculiar moisture which attaches to the brain.

63. Does the use of alcohol tend to increase crime and poverty?

Even its most strenuous advocates will not deny this fact, of which both statistics and common observation furnish abundant proofs. It has been estimated that four fifths of the pauperism and crime in our country result directly from strong drink.

238—1. Why does a laundress test the temperature of her flat-iron by holding it near her cheek?

The sense of warmth is very keen in the palms of the hand, the cheek, etc. This sensation is much less delicate in the lips and the back of the hand.

2. When we are cold, why do we spread the palms of our hands before the fire?

(See Question 1.)

3. What is meant by a "furred tongue"?

In health, the tongue has hardly a discernible lining, but in disease, the epithelium, or scarfskin, accumulates, and gives a white, coated appearance. This covering is likely to be of a yellowish shade when the liver is disturbed, and brown or dark in blood-diseases. One's occupation often colors it. Thus it is said the tongue of a tea-taster has a curious orange-tint.

4. Why has sand or sulphur no taste?

They are insoluble in the saliva.

5. What was the origin of the word palatable?

The mistaken notion that the palate, or roof of the mouth, is the seat of the taste.

6. Why does a cold in the head injure the flavor of our coffee?

Because the sense of taste is so dependent on that of smell.

7. Name some so-called flavors which are really sensations of touch.

(See *Physiology*, p. 348.)

Taste is not a simple sense. Certain other sensations, as those of touch, temperature, smell, and pain, are blended with it; and certain so-called tastes are really sensations of another kind. Thus an astringent taste, like that of alum, is more properly an astringent feeling, and results from an impression made upon the nerves of touch, that ramify in the tongue. In like manner, the qualities known as smooth, oily, watery, and mealy tastes, are dependent upon these same nerves of touch. A burning or pungent taste is a sensation of pain, having its seat in the tongue and throat. A cooling taste, like that of mint, pertains to that modification of touch called the sense of temperature.—HUTCHISON's *Physiology*, pp. 190, 191.

8. What is the object of the hairs in the nostrils?

They prevent the entrance of dust and other impurities. They are also exceedingly delicate in all sensations of touch.

9. What use does the nose subserve in the process of respiration?

It warns us of noxious gases, sifts out impurities, and tempers the air before it enters the delicate respiratory organs.

10. Why do we sometimes hold the nose when we take unpleasant medicine?

(See Question 6.)

11. Why is the nose placed over the mouth?

As a sentinel at the gate-way to the stomach and the lungs.

12. Describe how the hand is adapted to be the instrument of touch.

Its isolation at the extremity of the movable arm, the mobility of its different parts, and the delicacy of the sensation at the tips of the fingers, exquisitely adapt the hand to be the instrument of touch.

13. Besides being the organ of taste, what use does the tongue subserve?

It aids in the mastication of the food and in speech.

14. Why is not the act of tasting complete until we swallow?

Because the organ of taste is located especially in the back part of the tongue and the soft palate.

15. Why do all things have the same flavor when one's tongue is "furred" by fever?

They are really tasteless. The tongue is then dry, and there is no saliva to dissolve and carry particles of the food into the cells covering the nerves of taste.

16. Which sense is the more useful, hearing or sight?

(See *Wonders of the Human Body*, p. 201.)

"The sight speaks more directly to the intelligence; it enlarges the field of thought, it gives birth to precise notions of light, of form, of extent; and it permits the communication of thought by conventional signs. Hearing is a necessary condition of articulate language; without it man lives alone, affection and confidence lose their most precious forms of expression, and friendship can not exist. Auditory sensations act upon the nervous system with more force than visual sensations. We are carried away by rhythm, or it adapts itself to our ideas and our passions; music plunges us into an ideal world, and holds us by an indefinable charm; in a word, if sight speaks more especially to the intellect, hearing addresses itself to the affections. Sight is certainly more necessary to man than hearing, but still the blind are generally gay and communicative, while the deaf seem inclined to melancholy. As to the relative influence of these two senses on the development of the intellect, we know that the education of the deaf is slow, but may be complete, while that of the blind is, on the contrary, rather rapid, but is almost always very limited; many ideas can not be acquired by them, and, as has been remarked by M. Longet, their minds rarely attain maturity."

17. Which coat is the white of the eye?

The sclerotic.

18. What makes the difference in the color of eyes?

The varying shade of the pigment deposited in the iris of the eye.

19. Why do we snuff the air when we wish to obtain a distinct smell?

As muscular actions are called into play to aid the sense of taste, as in smacking the tongue and lips, so the act of "sniffing," which is a mixed respiratory and nasal muscular effort, is used to bring odorous substances more surely and extensively into contact with the upper and proper olfactory region of the nose, besides causing a larger amount of them to pass over the mucous surface in a given time.—MARSHALL.

20. Why do red-hot iron and frozen mercury ($-40°$) produce the same sensation?

The sensation in both cases is that of pain, not that of touch.

21. Why can an elderly person drink tea which to a child would be unbearably hot?

The sensation of touch has become impaired, and is much less delicate.

22. Why does an old man hold his paper so far from his eyes?

"Far sight" is common among elderly people, and is remedied by convex glasses. In old age the power of adjusting the crystalline lens is lost.

23. Would you rather be punished on the tips of your fingers than on the palm of your hand?

The sense of touch is much keener in the tips of the fingers than in the palm of the hand.

24. What is the object of the eyebrows? Are the hairs straight?

They serve to prevent the perspiration of the forehead from running down into the eye. They act, in a measure, with the eyelashes, also to screen the eye from the dust and glaring light. The hairs of the eyebrows overlap each other, and are set obliquely outward.

25. What is the use of winking?

It serves to wash the eyeballs, and thus keep the "windows of the soul" clean. The necessity for winking is shown by the great effort required to restrain it even for a short time. First discomfort, then congestion of the mucous membrane, and then a profuse watering of the eye follow any attempt at stopping this necessary act. It is an obscure sense of discomfort, not usually noticed by the consciousness, that excites this movement, the objects of which are periodically to cleanse the exposed part of the eyeball, to moisten and lubricate it with the secretions from the neighboring glands, and probably in this way to aid in the preservation of the polish and translucency of the epithelial layer on the transparent portion of the globe. At the same time it carries toward the inner corner all foreign bodies, and directs the residual secretions toward the lachrymal ducts. Finally, it allows a brief but periodical rest to the levator muscle of the upper eyelid.—MARSHALL.

26. When you wink, do the eyelids touch at once along their whole length? Why?

In winking, both lids move, but the upper one much the more extensively. Moreover, they do not come in contact all along their margins at the same instant of time, but meet first at the outer corner, and then rapidly inward as far as the lachrymal papillæ, on which the lachrymal ducts are situated. By this sweeping movement, all foreign bodies are carried to the lachrymal lake.—MARSHALL.

27. How many rows of hairs are there in the eyelashes?

The *eyelashes*, or *cilia*, consist of two, and opposite the middle of the eyelid, of three rows of finely-curved hairs—those of the upper lid being more numerous, thicker, and longer than those of the lower lid. "Those of the upper lid are curved upward, those of the lower lid are curved downward; and when the lids are brought near together, these two ranges of hairs stand like so many crossed sabers, or a kind of *chevaux-de-frise*, guarding the entrance to the eye."—DALTON'S *Physiology*, p. 330.

28. Do all nations have eyes of the same shape?

No. Witness the almond-shaped eyes of the Chinese. "The greater or less extent of the opening of the lids makes the eye appear larger or smaller; the conformation of the palpebral muscles and the tarsal cartilages gives to the eye an elongated and languishing form, as in the East, or round and bold, as among the Occidentals; but the dimensions and form of the globe are the same in all countries and in all individuals."—*Wonders of the Human Body*.

29. Why does snuff-taking cause a flow of tears?

Because of the action of the sympathetic system.

30. Why does a fall cause one to "see stars"? *

Whenever a nerve is excited in any way, it gives rise to the sensation peculiar to the organ with which it communicates. Thus, an electric shock sent through the eye gives rise to the appearance of a flash of light; and pressure on any part of the retina produces a luminous image, which lasts as long as the pressure, and is called a *phosphene*. If the point of the finger be pressed upon the outer side of the ball of the eye, a luminous image—which, in my own case, is dark in the center, with a bright ring at the circumference (or, as Newton described it, like the "eye" in a peacock's tail)—is seen; and this image lasts as long as the pressure is continued.—HUXLEY.

31. Why can we not see with the nose, or smell with the eyes?

Each set of nerves is adapted to transmit to the brain a peculiar class of sensations alone.

32. What causes the roughness of a cat's tongue?

The sharpness and strength of the papillæ upon its tongue. This is a peculiarity of the lion tribe.

33. Is the cuticle essential to touch?

Yes. If the cuticle be removed, as in case of a blister, contact with the exposed surface produces pain rather than a sense of touch.

34. Can one tickle himself?

It is said not; but the author has found persons who averred that they could produce this sensation upon themselves. The sense, it is noticeable, is present only in those parts where that of touch is feeble.

---

* On the occasion of a remarkable trial in Germany, it was claimed by a person who had been severely assaulted on a very dark night, that the flashes of light caused by repeated blows upon the head enabled him to see with sufficient distinctness to recognize his assailant. But the evidence of scientific men entirely refuted this claim, by pronouncing that the eye, under the circumstances named, was incapacitated for vision.—HUTCHISON.

35. Why does a bitter taste often produce vomiting?

The fifth pair of nerves, which supplies the lip and sides of the tongue, and perceives especially sweet and sour substances, ramifies over the face, and hence an acid will "pucker" the features; while the ninth pair, at the base of the tongue, which is sensitive to salt and bitter tastes, is distributed also to the throat, and is in sympathy with the internal organs, since it seems to be "a common nerve of feeling for the mucous membrane generally."

36. Is there any danger of looking "cross-eyed" for fun?

The muscles used thus in sport may become permanently distorted.

37. Should school-room desks face a window?

No. The light should be admitted so as to fall over the shoulder upon the book. Many school-rooms are arranged to accommodate the teacher only, while a blinding flood of light pours directly into the faces of the pupils.

38. Why do we look at a person to whom we are listening attentively?

One sense instinctively aids another.

39. Do we really feel with our fingers?

No. All sensation is in the mind.

40. Is the eye a perfect sphere?

No. The front projects somewhat, while, at the back, the optic nerve is attached like the stem to a fruit.

41. How often do we wink?

Five or six times a minute.

42. Why is the interior of a telescope or microscope often painted black?

To absorb the scattered rays of light which would confuse the vision. For the same reason, the posterior surface of the iris, the ciliary processes, and the choroid, are covered with a layer of dark pigment.

43. What is "the apple of the eye"?
The pupil.

44. What form of glasses do old people require?
(See Question 22.)

45. Should we ever wash our ears with cold water?
Rarely, if ever, lest we chill this sensitive organ.

46. What is the object of the winding passages in the nose?
To furnish additional surface on which to expand the olfactory nerve.

47. Can a smoker tell in the dark, whether or not his cigar is lighted?
Sight often seems to be essential to perfect what we call a sensation of taste.

48. Will a nerve re-unite after it has been cut?
Nerve-fiber seems to re-unite as readily as muscle-fiber.

49. Will the sight give us an idea of solidity?
(See *Physiology*, p. 247, note.)

50. Why can a skillful surgeon determine the condition of the brain and other internal organs by examining the interior of the eye?
(See *Physiology*, p. 248, note.)

51. Is there any truth in the idea that the image of the murderer can be seen in the eye of the dead victim?
When the flame of a taper is held near and a little on one side of a person's eye, any one looking into the eye from a proper point of view will see three images of the flame, two upright and one inverted. One upright figure is reflected from the front of the cornea, which acts as a convex mirror. The

second proceeds from the front of the crystalline lens, which has the same effect; while the inverted image proceeds from the posterior face of the lens, which, being convex backward, is, of course, concave forward, and acts as a concave mirror.—HUXLEY. The images formed upon the retina are as fleeting as light itself, from the nature of the case, and disappear as soon as the object is removed.

www.ingramcontent.com/pod-product-compliance
Lightning Source LLC
Chambersburg PA
CBHW031818220426
43662CB00007B/700